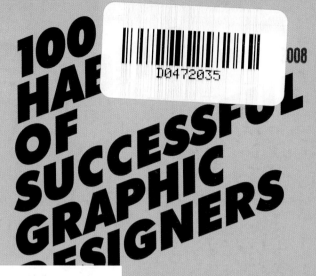

100
HAB
OF
SUCCESSFUL
GRAPHIC
DESIGNERS

008

ROCKPORT

© 2003 by Rockport Publishers, Inc.

First paperback edition printed 2005.

First published in the United States of America by
Rockport Publishers, Inc., a member of
Quayside Publishing Group
33 Commercial Street
Gloucester, Massachusetts 01930-5089
Telephone: (978) 282-9590
Fax: (978) 283-2742
www.rockpub.com

Library of Congress Cataloging-in-Publication Data available

ISBN-13: 978-1-59253-188-2
ISBN-10: 1-59253-188-1

10 9 8 7 6

Design: Joshua Berger / Plazm
Copyeditor: Pamela Elizian
Proofreader: Sarah T. Chaffee
Cover concept by Pete McCracken

Printed in China

100 HABITS OF SUCCESSFUL GRAPHIC DESIGNERS

INSIDER SECRETS ON WORKING SMART AND STAYING CREATIVE

ROCKPORT
PUBLISHERS

WRITTEN AND DESIGNED BY PLAZM

WRITING BY SARAH DOUGHER

DESIGN BY JOSHUA BERGER

Contents

Introduction   8

Chapter 1. Self-Promotion   10
Chapter 2. Working with Clients   36
Chapter 3. Workflow and In-House Dynamics   60
Chapter 4. Continuing Education and Professional Development   84
Chapter 5. Community Involvement   102
Chapter 6. Technology   124
Chapter 7. Personal Growth and Keeping Creativity Alive   146
Chapter 8. Partnerships and Strategic Synergies   170

Chapter 1. Self-Promotion page 10

1   Let the work speak for itself
    Stefan Sagmeister
2   Create promotions that reflect the goals of your company
    Mark Randall, Worldstudio, Inc.
3   Keep in touch with your clients, past and present
    Why Not Associates
4   Let someone publish your work
    Art Chantry
5   Win and keep clients with a multi-pronged approach to
    self-promotion
    Margo Chase, Chase Design Group
6   Use cultural relevance to create ongoing momentum
    John C Jay, Wieden+Kennedy, Tokyo
7   Create self-promotional materials that are deceptively
    simple
    Worksight
8   Do an extra-good job on tiny projects
    Worksight
9   Distribute your work through respected channels to gain
    client confidence
    Hideki Nakajima
10 Everything you do promotes yourself
    Miles Murray Sorrell FUEL
11 Walk around a book fair and hand out your book designs
    to publishers
    Worksight
12 Create after-the-fact flyers
    Ed Fella

Chapter 2. Working with Clients page 36

13 Visit the client's site—physical and virtual
    Stefan Sagmeister
14 Research client decision-making systems
    Worldstudio, Inc.
15 Spend time with your client to build consensus and create
    shared goals
    John C Jay, Wieden+Kennedy, Tokyo
16 Expand your audience by doing public art projects
    Why Not Associates
17 Don't talk about CD art in a CD art meeting
    Stefan Sagmeister
18 All work has its own unique client
    Miles Murray Sorrell FUEL
19 Learn the language of the client
    Todd Waterbury, Wieden+Kennedy, New York
20 Teach the client your language
    Todd Waterbury, Wieden+Kennedy, New York
21 Seek out creative clients for successful collaborations
    Margo Chase, Chase Design Group
22 Build small projects into engaging, ongoing work
    Worksight
23 Work for the government
    Why Not Associates
24 Develop a clear ethic of client interaction that works
    for you
    Stefan Sagmeister

Chapter 3. Workflow and In-House Dynamics page 60

25 Find an emotional connection with your audience
   Todd Waterbury, Wieden+Kennedy, New York
26 Demand respect, creative license, and fair pay
   Art Chantry
27 Expand with your clients
   Worldstudio, Inc.
28 Develop brands that both reflect and influence culture
   Todd Waterbury, Wieden+Kennedy, New York
29 Help save electricity
   Miles Murray Sorrell FUEL
30 If you are a designer, design; if you are a manager,
   manage
   Stefan Sagmeister
31 Accessible can be smart; smart can be funny
   Why Not Associates
32 Hire interesting, creative people—and listen to them
   John C Jay, Wieden+Kennedy, Tokyo
33 Always keep the valve in the open position
   Miles Murray Sorrell FUEL
34 Cultivate a workplace with a specific look and sound
   Margo Chase, Chase Design Group
35 Keep decision making simple and nonhierarchical
   Why Not Associates
36 Creative directors need to stay creative
   John C Jay, Studio J
37 Look far and wide for your sources in the creative process
   Margo Chase, Chase Design Group

Chapter 4. Continuing Education and Professional Development page 84

38 Avoid design conferences
   Stefan Sagmeister
39 Support young designers
   Worksight
40 When you retire, deal with the possibilities, not the
   necessities
   Ed Fella
41 Go back to school no matter how old you are
   Ed Fella
42 Start a magazine
   Rudy VanderLans and Zuzana Licko, Emigre
43 Make a low-budget project look expensive
   Chase Design Group
44 Read it all, forget it all, and do your own thing
   Rudy VanderLans and Zuzana Licko, Emigre
45 Actively pursue intellectual subjects that resonate with you
   Worksight
46 Learn the vernacular of a new field
   Worksight
47 Continue your own education by teaching
   Chase Design Group
48 Develop and sustain an art practice throughout your life
   Ed Fella
49 Never stop learning; don't start teaching
   Miles Murray Sorrell FUEL
50 Encourage young people to make art
   John C Jay, Wieden+Kennedy, Tokyo

Chapter 5. Community Involvement page 102

51 Develop a social agenda
    Mark Randall, Worldstudio, Inc., Worldstudio Foundation
52 Develop long-term relationships with nonprofit organizations
    Stefan Sagmeister
53 Address local, immediate needs
    Mark Randall, Worldstudio, Inc.
54 Use the Robin Hood theory
    Ed Fella
55 Minimize travel expenses—work with your neighbors
    Miles Murray Sorrell FUEL
56 Create highly visible and culturally consequential design
    by working for clients in education and the arts
    John C Jay, Wieden+Kennedy, Tokyo
57 Integrate your politics with your creation
    Rudy VanderLans and Zuzana Licko, Emigre
58 Teach
    Worksight
59 Don't feel obligated to do charity work
    Chase Design Group
60 Keep in touch with your nonprofit clients
    Worksight
61 Partner with like-minded firms
    Worksight
62 Use client work to collaborate with young new artists
    John C Jay, Wieden+Kennedy, Tokyo
63 Provide service to your design community
    Worksight

Chapter 6. Technology page 124

64 Acknowledge the value of the analog process
    Hideki Nakajima
65 Use computers to communicate with stone masons
    Why Not Associates
66 Make design invisible
    Todd Waterbury, Wieden+Kennedy, New York
67 Recognize the limits of digital technology for creative work
    Ed Fella
68 Let your small shop thrive on high-tech
    Worksight
69 Whatever you think, technology is in control
    Miles Murray Sorrell FUEL
70 Remember that technology serves you; you do not serve
    technology
    Chase Design Group
71 Use technology in unexpected ways
    Why Not Associates
72 Work with emerging technologies
    Rudy VanderLans and Zuzana Licko, Emigre
73 Make friends with people who know a technology that
    you want to learn
    Why Not Associates
74 Develop an overarching technology metaphor
    Worksight
75 It's OK to not go multimedia
    Worksight
76 Use the computer as a business tool as well as a
    creative tool
    Rudy VanderLans and Zuzana Licko, Emigre

About the Contributors 190

Andy Altman, Why Not Associates
Art Chantry, Art Chantry Design
Margo Chase, Chase Design Group
Ed Fella
John C Jay, Wieden+Kennedy, Tokyo
Miles Murray Sorrell FUEL
Hideki Nakajima, Nakajima Design
Mark Randall, World Studio Foundation/ Worldstudio Inc.
Stefan Sagmeister, Sagmeister Studio
Scott Santoro, Worksight
Rudy VanderLans and Zuzana Licko, Emigre
Todd Waterbury, Wieden+Kennedy, New York

About the Author and Designer 192

Chapter 7. Personal Growth and Keeping Creativity Alive
page 146

77 Travel as much as possible
    Mark Randall, Worldstudio, Inc.
78 Look at the everyday world for inspiration
    Worksight
79 Watch videos of comedians
    Why Not Associates
80 Practice and preach, don't theorize and teach
    Ed Fella
81 Change your environment
    Art Chantry
82 Have conversations with great talents
    Hideki Nakajima
83 Keep creativity alive by any means
    Miles Murray Sorrell FUEL
84 Read a good book
    Margo Chase
85 Set up shop in a foreign country during a recession
    John C Jay, Wieden+Kennedy, Tokyo
86 Work with visual artists
    Todd Waterbury, Wieden+Kennedy, New York
87 Take some time off
    Stefan Sagmeister
88 Develop personal growth and personal taste; you are
    what you eat
    Miles Murray Sorrell FUEL
89 Take risks with your career
    John C Jay, Wieden+Kennedy Tokyo

Chapter 8. Partnerships and Strategic Synergies page 170

90 The secret of a successful partnership is to never
    compromise
    Miles Murray Sorrell FUEL
91 Collaborate with someone in a different field
    Stefan Sagmeister
92 Collaborate with someone whose skills complement
    your own
    Art Chantry
93 Collaboration does not depend on compromise but
    rather on good decisions about whom you work with
    Rudy VanderLans and Zuzana Licko, Emigre
94 Find a mutually beneficial relationship
    Mark Randall, Worldstudio Foundation
95 Allow each creative team to determine its collaborative
    approach
    Todd Waterbury, Wieden+Kennedy, New York
96 Take a risk in choosing collaborative partners
    Worksight
97 Partner with companies willing to take risks
    Art Chantry
98 Partner with civic organizations
    Why Not Associates
99 Forge partnerships that broaden your cultural horizons
    Chase Design Group
100 Help other people collaborate
    Worldstudio Foundation

Introduction

Although many designers encounter similar challenges in their work, the ways in which they meet these challenges are what differentiates one designer from another. Each designer in this book goes about his or her craft in a different, highly idiosyncratic manner, and yet each style of work gives us insight into the larger problem of process and, ultimately, of creative work. The observations offered in this book range from the practical to the theoretical, and where one reader might find affinity with a suggestion, another might find it absurd.

In her monograph *Make It Bigger*, Paula Scher writes about magazine editorial design and suggests that most magazines fall into either the "coping" category or the "craving" category. "Coping magazines tend to have lots of instructional information. It is often completely useless, but it looks didactic all the same… Craving magazines tend toward big, splashy, dramatic layouts of photographs filled with people, places, and stuff." This differentiation is useful because it delineates the graphic style and editorial content. It also presents a model that can encompass graphic and editorial environments outside the magazine by suggesting two categories of consuming information: *I want to know how to do it* and *I want it*. Many design books fall into these two categories as well—we are familiar with textbook-style how-to books, as well as flashy monographs from established designers and firms.

In the initial stages of developing this book, we fought hard against writing a book that depended on the coping model for its content and presentation. The designers we interviewed had so much more to offer the reader than practical information about how to do design. Their insights often worked against the idea that anyone could learn or teach design, because commercial contexts vary so greatly, and the range of designers we interviewed worked in such different contexts. Sometimes *I want to know how to do it* merges with *I want it* in subtle and interesting ways. It was obvious to us that we needed to translate these ideas into a book that would be useful to readers.

In this book, Plazm presents 11 designers from North America, Japan, and the United Kingdom, whose complexity of thought and execution puts them at the top of the graphic design world. Our text presents their high level of knowledge in a clearly written and well-illustrated format. Eight chapters provide a comprehensive picture of the elements required to successfully run a design studio, from client interaction to the process of continuing education. We are also pleased to present some of the designers' newest and most exciting projects. Through the use of highlighted ideas culled from interviews, designers provide insight into their thoughts and approaches to the business and art of design.

By breaking the process of graphic design down into design-related subjects and subjects related to the business of design work, we hope to bring the reader a book that acknowledges both the practical and the creative aspects of graphic design. The way a designer runs his or her shop can show as much creativity as the way he or she goes about creating a logo—these creative challenges are linked and the tools for their solutions often come from similar sources.

We selected the designers for this book because they represent a range of styles and situations. We demonstrate the variety of methods that designers use to solve problems—how the same issue might be dealt with in a large or small office, how decisions are made, or how the chain of command handled it in an entirely different context. Their contributions to this book are a testament to the energy that propels the design field at the start of the new millennium.

                    —Sarah Dougher

Self-Promotion
01-12

Self-promotion puts the message about the artist's work out into the world. At their best, self-promotional campaigns attract clients and act as an effective business-development tool. Many of the designers we talked to don't use what might be described as overt self-promotional tools—they don't create brochures or other materials to directly address potential clients. Rather, they find ways to let the power of their work speak for itself and let the clients come to them. This is an ideal position to find oneself in, but, especially in difficult economic times, it has become increasingly rare. Although some designers would not necessarily call what they do self-promotion, anything that is done to increase the public image and reputation of a designer or firm can be considered self-promotion.

Self-promotion is intimately tied to the creation of a designer's strongest work and its distribution into the world. Any designer who has done advertising knows that if the product does not deliver, the ad cannot make it deliver, no matter how clever and attractive the ad may be. Designers with effective self-promotional strategies use what they design to promote themselves in a variety of ways, from giving away CDs featuring their packaging to creating a magazine that uses only their own fonts. In such ways, designers not only can show off the effectiveness of their designs, but can also place their work into the context of a larger culture.

① Let the work speak for itself

MAK poster
Stefan Sagmeister

Stefan Sagmeister has never bothered to do any self-promotion, save a change-of-address-style postcard when he opened his new shop in New York. "We basically don't do any self-initiated self-promotion. We haven't even done a Christmas card, ever. We have never sent out a press release, ever." Despite this fact, Sagmeister consistently has to turn clients away.

This admonition also belies the fact that Sagmeister does not actively create self-promotional materials to gain business; rather, he uses his design work to promote himself, creating posters for talks that he gives in New York and around the world, such as the one shown here for the Viennese museum, MAK. He considers these projects to be client work, because he does not pay for the materials or printing, yet he is able to render something new that is associated with both him and the talk he is giving. These posters actively add value to Sagmeister, whether the viewer associates them with the man or the studio.

In addition, Sagmeister participates in design shows but has never created work solely for this purpose.

Sagmeister CD design work is prolific. He often asks the client for a hundred or so finished CDs to send to friends and clients—sort of a self-promotional gift. "We send them out to get work and also to friends at other labels. But we basically send out the CD and a letter, so that people in the street know what we just did. That's been working quite well for us. Because we try to design packaging for music we like, most of the CDs we package have good music."

Designer: Stefan Sagmeister

2 Create promotions that reflect the goals of your company

Worldstudio promotional mailers
Mark Randall, Worldstudio, Inc.

Worldstudio, Inc., keeps in touch with its clients by sending them thank-you cards and a fancy box of chocolates at the end of the year. In the note, they thank clients for their business and remind them that 10 percent of the proceeds from every job goes to the Worldstudio Foundation, their socially progressive, nonprofit organization. They highlight the Foundation's activities that year, giving clients a chance to recognize that they have helped without even realizing it. It is one of the only times that the clients of Worldstudio, Inc., hear about the activities of the Worldstudio Foundation. Otherwise, the partners keep the messaging about each entity as separate as possible. Randall says, "In the very beginning, we were really keen on merging Worldstudio, Inc., and Worldstudio Foundation by describing that we are a graphic design studio and a foundation, and we care about our community and all of that. Not to be callous or mean about it, but basically, clients don't care. It's like, 'Oh yeah, that's nice, but what about my brochure?' Or 'I need a

new logo,' or 'it's costing too much,' or 'I need that sooner.' They appreciate the fact that we do this, but it is not a deciding factor why people work with us."

The mission of the Worldstudio Foundation remains central to the principals of Worldstudio, Inc. In creating promotional materials for clients, it is important to them to make a strong statement about the identity of their firm, despite the fact that it may not have much impact on business development.

Designers: Mark Randall, David Sterling

③ Keep in touch with your clients, past and present

Ecstacity
Why Not Associates

Why Not's success has created the enviable situation in which they have never had to seek out work. Instead, their self-promotion has consisted of maintaining close client connections to keep the work coming in. Andy Altmann of Why Not notes, "This year has been the quietest we've ever had, and we've been like, 'How do you get work?' So we checked with all the clients we have ever worked with in the past, and that's worked, so now we are busy again. It the past, we've been quite blasé about it, but it is a little different now. We are doing a lot of repeat work for existing clients, but that is not new work, exactly. A lot of going through the motions, but that is what keeps food on the table. The more interesting projects don't come along as frequently."

In 1992, Why Not Associates designed the catalog for a Nigel Coates exhibition of architectural drawings and ideas, which was shown at the Architectural Association in London. The subject of this project was the development of a mythical city, which was like a large body, living and breathing and interacting with its inhabitants. A few years later, Coates appached Why Not because he wanted to extend this idea to create what amounted to a guide book of this mythical city as a means of discussing the state of city planning.

Although the job has stretched out for a number of years, the book will be published this fall. Working with an architect from the initial stages of an idea to the unique, book-form presentation has given Why Not a greater appreciation for the processes of architects, as well as a role in the organic development of a project—from a catalog to a book.

Author: Nigel Coates
Art Directors, Designers: Why Not Associates
Photography: various
Client: Lawrence King Publishers

If we've done our job correctly, this issue of *Folio:* is a slap in the face to sissy design. A finger in the eye of conformity. A dumdum bullet in the brain of the corporate. In other words, a loving tribute to the oeuvre of Art Chantry. For more than 20 years—as Seattle's unofficial grandaddy of grunge—Art has gone diving in the dumpsters of popular culture, and come up again and again with fresh ways to disturb the collective unconscious. Needless to say, we're honored to present his work here in all its elegant grit.

④ Let someone publish your work

Some People Can't Surf: The Graphic Design of Art Chantry
Art Chantry

Some designers, especially those who have been working for a number of years, have the opportunity to publish their collected work in a monograph. In 2001, Chronicle books published *Some People Can't Surf: The Graphic Design of Art Chantry*, an excellent introduction to Chantry's work written by Julie Lasky. "I've gotten a lot of mileage out of that book. It is a terrific piece of self-promotion, obviously. I think I can safely say that up until that book I didn't ever get any work out of self-promotion or magazine articles or anything like that. In fact, just the opposite is true. In the late '80s sometime, I was featured in CA [*Communication Arts*] and didn't work for nine months after that. Nothing. It did nothing."

Chantry notes, however, that in the design world, the monograph can also be the kiss of death for a career. Many of his colleagues advised him against doing it. He sees the monograph as a sort of stabilizer that demonstrates both the core and limits of a designer's capabilities. On the flip side, it can also create the perception that no one can afford to hire you anymore, that you are unavailable, or, at worst, dead. Thankfully, however, Chantry has proved this is not always the case. Chantry's other efforts at

self-promotion come primarily from collaborations with clients who want to advertise their own capabilities using Chantry's work. This collaboration generally results in showpieces and collectable posters.

Because so much of Chantry's work has been on ephemeral objects, like posters and flyers, a book like *Some People Can't Surf* preserves a vital piece of the history of the graphic design of '80s and '90s punk culture, so much of which is repeated and copied in contemporary underground (and mainstream) music culture. For every piece in the book, Chantry insists that there are ten that he didn't include—so vast is the backlog of his work. "I have enough for probably five more volumes," he notes.

Publishing a monograph is not an option for every designer, but in the event that one has the opportunity to do so, it provides an important showpiece for prospective clients—however ambivalent the designer may feel about it.

Designer: Art Chantry

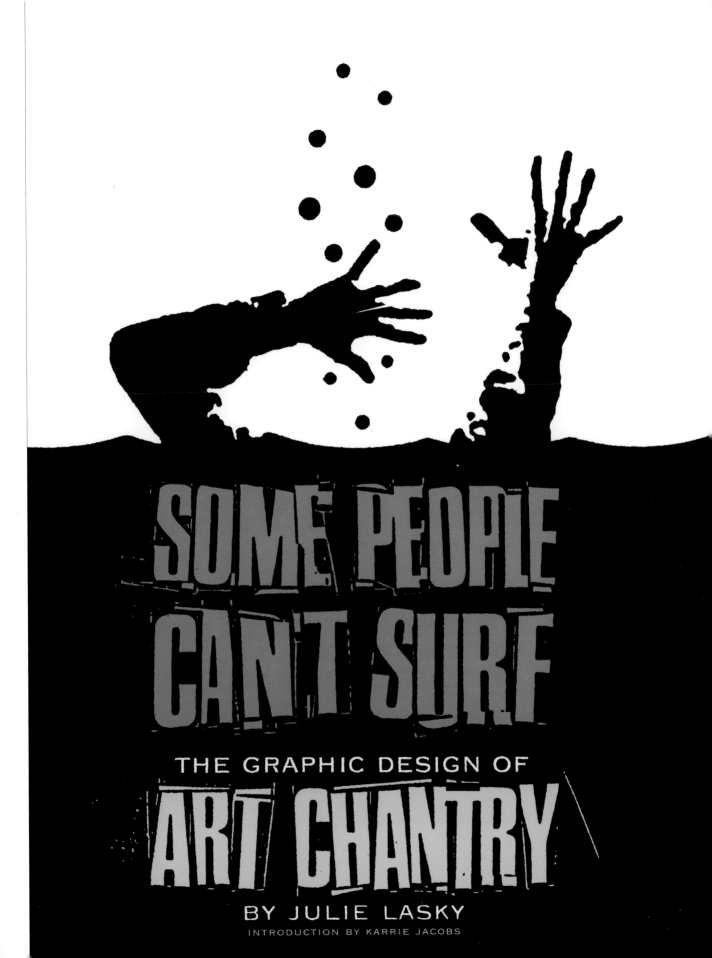

SOME PEOPLE CAN'T SURF

THE GRAPHIC DESIGN OF
ART CHANTRY

BY JULIE LASKY

INTRODUCTION BY KARRIE JACOBS

Folio: Art Chantry
Designer: Chuck Pennington
Copywriter: Palmer Petterson
Photography: Don Mason (posters), Chuck Pennington (Art Chantry)

Yes, it's Art Chantry, ladies and gentleman.

Art with a capital A. Let's have a big warm Seattle welcome for the rebel with the well-tuned xerox. The postmodern master of Sub Pop culture. Our poster boy for appropriation.

At the un-mellow age of 45, Art has already earned the admiration and emulation of the global design community. He's an International Poster Laureate, whose work has been shown in the Louvre, and hangs in the permanent collection of MOMA.

⑤ # Win and keep clients with a multi-pronged approach to self-promotion

Logo poster
Margo Chase, Chase Design Group

The Chase Design Group enters shows, such as those held by *Communication Arts, How,* and *Print,* and submits work to books as a way of self-promotion. In addition, they do occasional mailings that show their new work to specific types of clients. They also have an elaborate Web site on which they display a portfolio, a client list, and contact information.

Referral is a huge part of the Chase Design Group's business development, and it constitutes the means by which they get much of their new business. Maintaining a good account office is an essential part of this mechanism, almost as important as the work itself. Chase notes, "We are fortunate to have had ongoing work for many years with some clients. These are large and small corporations, as well as entertainment companies, where design plays a large role in their business. A lot depends on the type of client. If we do an identity for a company whose business does not involve design, they may not need us again for years, and by then, they may just want to try someone else. That part works in our favor also—people who have previously worked with others often call us to try something different."

The logo posters are a staple of the Chase Design Group's self-promotion, as well as an excellent catalog of their large and diverse client base. The one featured here is third in a series of three produced over the past ten years, each featuring 77 new logos. "The process of creating these has changed with technology," comments Chase. "The first poster we did was produced photomechanically, because it was created before we had our first Macintosh. The second poster included a few logos that were done by hand, but all were scanned into the computer. The third poster was built in Illustrator. Even the hand-done, calligraphic parts of the logos were streamlined or scanned to create digital art for all the logos."

Chase observes that industry recognition keeps her firm visible among people who recommend design firms, and the business press keeps her firm visible among clients and prospects; she acknowledges the power of both. Publicity, such as being featured in books or winning awards, is also an effective tool. "We get most of our nonreferral business from people who have seen our work in magazines or books. We often get referred by people who have never worked with us, but they know our work and reputation." In addition, Chase often speaks at design trade shows, which she enjoys, and which serves to keep industry awareness of her firm high. For Chase Design Group, a combination of approaches creates a flexible and effective self-promotional plan that reaches many different markets and potential clients.

Art Director: Margo Chase
Designers: Margo Chase, Brian Hunt, Jonathan Sample
Studio: Chase Design Group

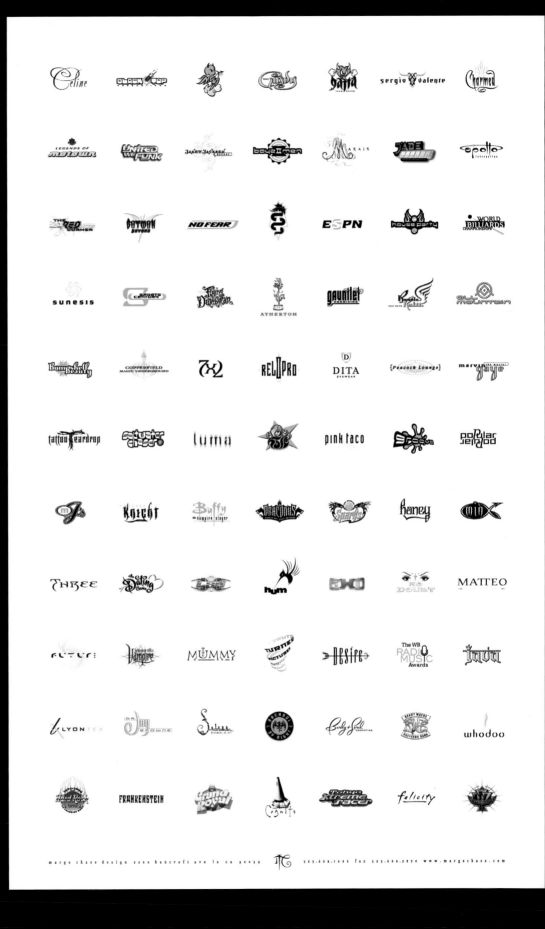

margo chase design 2255 bancroft ave la ca 90039 323.664.7955 fax 323.664.2970 www.margochase.com

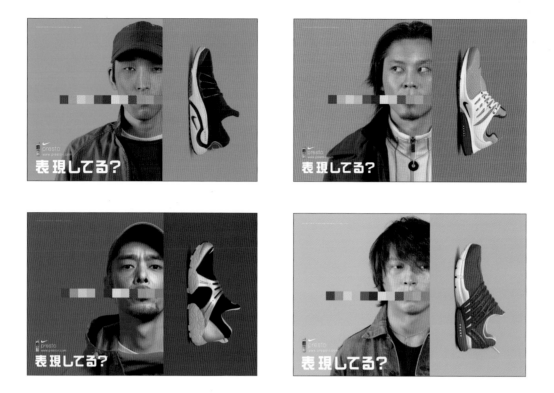

⑥ Use cultural relevance to create ongoing momentum

Presto 1: Emotions, Presto 2: Are you expressing?
John C Jay, Wieden+Kennedy, Tokyo

In developing the multilayered audio and video pieces to advertise the first products in a Nike shoe line called "Presto," John C Jay, creative director and partner at Wieden+Kennedy, Tokyo, wanted to create a momentum beyond what their work is able to do for the current product launch. "The things we make are never for sale," he comments. These can include special CDs, DVDs, or LPs. "We use them for special promotions, although promotions wouldn't be quite the right word. We use these things to make sure that key influencers of sports and society are continuously inspired by Nike's view of the world and Nike's dedication to helping young talent. Through Nike, we are supporting young talent and giving them a place to express themselves."

In addition to giving the brand momentum, such campaigns accrue cultural capital for their creators. Presto advertisements

tap into a social consciousness, as well as into a sports culture and a youth culture, establishing both Nike and Wieden+Kennedy as preeminent experts in these areas. The "Presto 1" campaign illustrates this concept well. The company's first pass at Presto involved the creation of an enhanced CD featuring five influential indie bands. "This campaign was in response to the whole 'indie' movement in youth culture–people playing indie sports, people leading an indie life, in the sense that they work toward a career that makes sense to them, not following the given path, the traditional path." For the print and outdoor advertising, Wieden+Kennedy asked musicians for an emotional response to the color of a given Presto shoe. In the second Presto campaign, Wieden+Kennedy engaged top DJs by featuring them in the advertising with a color bar over their mouths and the copy "Are you expressing?" on a special series of vinyl LPs. By finding the niche for a product and

FEED (Maya)
Genre: British Pop

Formed in Tokyo in 1994. Influencers from different fields have expressed unanimous admiration for Feed and they recently did an opening gig for theSmashing Pumpkins' Japan Tour '00. Their style goes beyond limits of Japanese music, taking a more international stance in their high quality music.

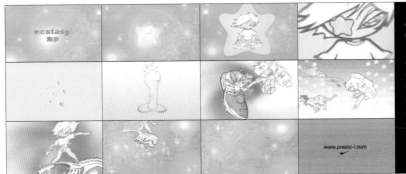

AOA (Hilah)
Genre: Trance/Techno

AOA is the representatitve Techno-Trance band in the Comma label. Their distinctive feature is that they play ad-lib by using live musical instruments such as percussion and guitars to play Techno-Trance. They rank top in College Radio Japan chart and they appear frequently at outdoor Rave style events. Performed at Presto event.

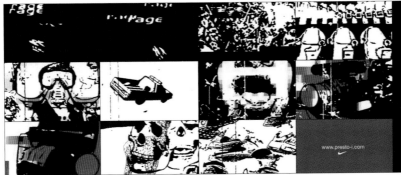

COALTAR OF THE DEEPERS (Narasaki)
Genre: Alternative rock

Formed in 1991, the band is one of the most popular Alternative rock bands on Indies label. Their dynamic yet sensitive sound revolves around Narasaki, their lead vocalist, and has been highly evaluated by the top musicians and music industry. Their core fans exist not only in Tokyo but all around the nation.

PEACE PILL (Tadanobu)
Genre: Alternative rock

Formed in Tokyo in 1991. An alternative rock band led by a painter, a musician but mostly known for as an actor Tadanobu Asano. Together with his partner Michimoro Iwaida, they produce free style and experimental music which is gaining high praise and respect in the Indies music scene.

communicating culturally appropriate messages about that product, Wieden+Kennedy not only demonstrate their skill in these conventional agency acts but also associate their firm with cutting-edge culture.

Another project (not illustrated here) that Wieden+Kennedy produced for Nike, "Players Delight," was created to celebrate the 20th anniversary of the emergence of hip hop and the release of "Rapper's Delight." Jay notes that the album is still for sale on the Internet, from anywhere between $700 to $1,000 dollars, and is still being played in top clubs. "That campaign did not die. It lived on and on. One of the things we are trying to do is to break all these rules of the status quo about what advertising is. So often ad agencies, and clients, in particular, just want to know what's next. There's no longevity of thought and brand extension. This is our fourth or fifth Presto launch, and each had a very dynamic, different type of idea."

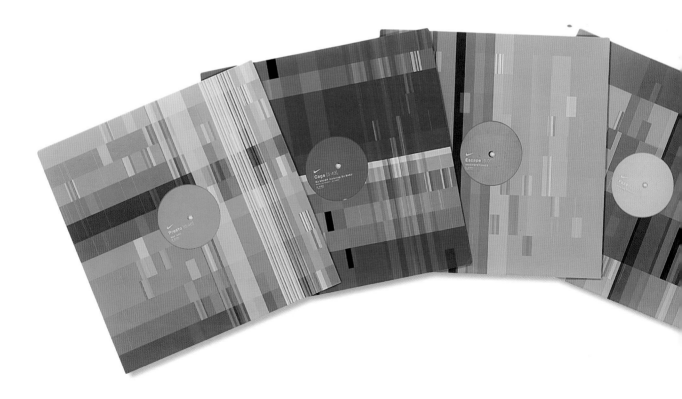

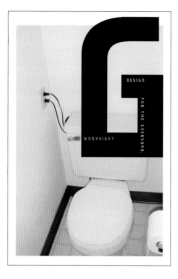

⑦ Create self-promotional materials that are deceptively simple

Self-promotional cards
Worksight

Worksight developed a series of postcards to illustrate the concept of "everyday design," which permeates their design philosophy. Scott Santoro explains, "They were experiments with the idea of the 'everyday' and functioned as promotional cards. They probably scared some people. Some people don't know what to make of them." Some of the photos are of trash or of scenes that do not immediately appeal in conventional aesthetic ways. Regardless of this fear, designers who come to Santoro's studio pick up the postcards as souvenirs of their visit. In addition, Santoro uses them to jot notes to clients—a highly decorated and conceptual form of stationery. "They are really just visual experiements based on my interest on the subject of the 'everyday' and how it relates to graphic design. However, they also function as promotional poscards for my studio. I suppose they might confuse people who don't know what to make of them, but that's OK."

The extension of this project is to make a bookmark. "We have a lot of publishing clients," says Santoro. "We think doing a bookmark would be an appropriate use of the idea for publishers. I'll get around to it one of these days."

Doing printed experiments can communicate aesthetics to potential clients as well as to colleagues in the business. They show a high degree of care for the small communication that happens on a daily basis, illustrating again the concept of the "everyday."

Designer: Scott Santoro/Worksight

⑧ Do an extra-good job on tiny projects

America the Beautiful cover
Worksight

To solicit new business, Scott Santoro of Worksight does the conventional work of making calls and networking through existing channels. But Santoro finds that the best way to create new business for himself is to start small and count on a bigger payoff down the road. "I'll try to do an extra-good job on tiny projects in the hopes that a company will grow and use me again. Sometimes it works. With a new client I'll work especially hard to design something that's smart and efficient. I guess I'm trying to prove my designing capabilities to them."

A publisher called Publicaffairs hired Worksight to design its catalog and then a book. The publisher grew and asked Worksight to redesign the catalog. Now Worksight produces it every three months. It started as what Santoro calls a "quickie catalog design" four years ago and has now turned into solid business every three months.

Eventually, Publicaffairs asked Santoro to design a book called *America the Beautiful*, a book by Lynn Sherr on the history of Katherine Bates's turn-of-the-century poem turned song. Doing a complex project such as designing a book was certainly a step up from the previous catalog work. Scott has found that the strategy of starting small works for publishers in general. "If we get a book project, usually I'll try to work my butt off to get something designed really smartly or efficiently. I guess that is the hope of all designers."

Sometimes this strategy backfires, leaving the designer with a great portfolio piece but not much more in the way of new business. Worksight designed an identity and a Web site for a small start-up dot-com company. After the Web site was done, the company kept the logo but then asked the new president's son to redo the Web site. Even though this project ended up not leading to other projects, it was important for Santoro to do a good job on it. In the larger body of work of a designer, it is essential to pay attention to detail, even on the smallest projects, because this work can have a life beyond the client, to both fuel the imagination and provide portfolio material.

Designer: Scott Santoro/Worksight
Client: Publicaffairs

⑨ Distribute your work through respected channels to gain client confidence

Revival, 57 Images from Cut Magazine
Hideki Nakajima

Hideki Nakajima has published two books that feature most of his work. He finds them useful for establishing credibility with his prospective clients. The books also serve as his portfolio for exhibitions in which he is asked to participate. "Two books that collect my works are titled *Revival* and *Nakajima Design 1995-2000*. I also did the exhibition 'New Village/Code Exhibition' (2002). The magazine *IDEA* had a special feature on my work in 2000 as well."

Most of Nakajima's clients come to him over and over, so he has little need to self-promote. On the other hand, he also believes that award shows and competitions give his clients a sense of security, a validation by the design establishment that his work is recognized by his peers. For Nakajima, his reputation is built on his work and through the books and articles that feature his work. In developing a body of published work, Nakajima effectively creates a stand-in for what a conventional designer might use as a portfolio. His books are designed *as* books, created to stand alone as pieces of work in themselves.

Art Director: Hideki Nakajima
Design: Hideki Nakajima
Photography: Takuya Imamura, Shigemi Tsutsumi, Itaru Hirama
Client: Rockin' On

Ethan Hawke

Breaking up with someone is almost like a death.

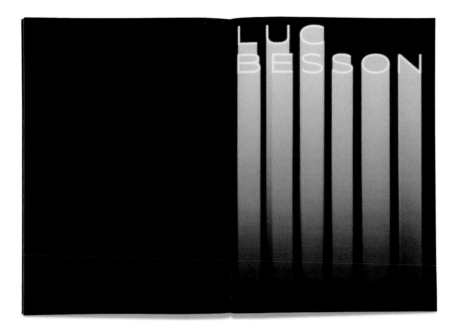

Everything you do promotes yourself

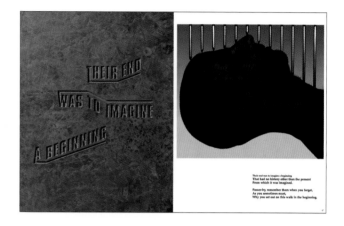

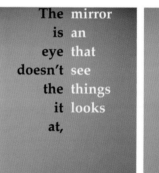

Fuel 3000 cover, spreads
Miles Murray Sorrell FUEL

Miles Murray Sorrell FUEL began by publishing experimental magazines. "The publication of our own magazines and books is the foundation of our business. The books' broader distribution gained us a wider audience and subsequently helped to attract commissions," notes Damon Murray, one of Miles Murray Sorrell FUEL's partners. (The other partners are Peter Miles and Stephen Sorrell.)

The majority of Miles Murray Sorrell FUEL's work comes by way of referral, and they do not do any advertising or self-promotion per se. "The starting point for our personal work is not primarily to gain more commercial work. Often our personal work is too difficult to grasp in a commercial environment," explains Murray. Miles Murray Sorrell FUEL's client list of artists and other designers reflects the complex nature of their personal projects. This philosophy has created a situation where FUEL's client base is populated by artists as well, including photographer Jürgen Teller, Booth Clibborn Editions (who published both of their books), and fashion designer Marc Jacobs.

Designers: Miles Murray Sorrell FUEL
Client: Booth Clibborn Editions

⑪ Walk around a book fair and hand out your book designs to publishers

The Sea Around Us cover
Worksight

The combination of a lagging economy and some do-it-yourself pluck provided the circumstances for a novel business development tool: hitting the pavement. Scott Santoro of Worksight knew that he wanted more business with book publishers, so he decided to go ask them if they needed his services.

"I heard that there was a book-publishers' fair down at the Javits [Convention] Center. I thought, that would be a great place to bring laser prints of my book work. I'll walk around until I see books that I like. I'll walk right up to the people representing the company and tell them that I am a book designer and ask them if they could hand these off to the art director. I handed out about 30 copies at a fair that had about 300 publishers. I ended up getting some nice work from it."

The strategy of direct self-promotion at a book fair was effective for Worksight. One of the clients he gleaned through this jaunt through the convention center was Oxford University Press. They called him on the strength of the lasers that he handed out, and he was able to get an excellent project as a result. They were reprinting Rachel Carson's book, *The Sea Around Us*, which was first published in 1951. It was the 50-year anniversary of the first edition, one of the first environmentally oriented books written about the sea, and Oxford wanted a special treatment.

Designer: Scott Santoro/Worksight
Client: Oxford University Press

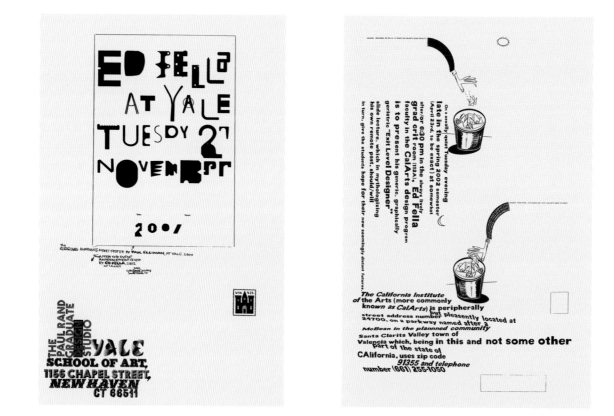

⑫ Create after-the-fact flyers

Announcement Flyers
Ed Fella

To complement his typographic experimentation, Ed Fella started experimenting with direct mail advertisements, or flyers. He began creating what he calls "after-the-fact" announcements, which function as a souvenir for the event they advertise. "The one I'm doing now is from a lecture I did at Yale University in November 2001, so I'm just now working on the flyer. I'll print it—a couple hundred copies, that's it. They become a kind of idea about art design and art practice. Those other ones that advertise, they function as real flyers—they print a couple thousand of them and mail them out. I would just get my 'cut,' 50 copies or so. The whole idea of what I'm doing now is to just print the designer's cut, not the announcement—just do an edition."

In the poster shown here, Fella combines sports lettering from Yale with odd kinds of old-fashioned lettering, creating a look of sports nostalgia mixed with thoughtful graphic design. The result is an eclectic mix that has nothing to do with the present. Fella notes, "I guess it's a kind of post-modernism. These pieces function autonomously. They don't function in the design world; they occasionally make it into the art world, into a gallery or a museum. The posters that I do are very specific to a very small

audience. The Yale poster won't make any sense to anyone besides people who are involved with the Yale graphic design program. They will be the ones to get the nuances. Yet it works as a piece, an announcement. It's readable; it gives you the time and the place of the event."

All graphic design announces something: it is worthless after the event is over. Fella's philosophy of the edition drives him to create these seemingly obsolete pieces. "I make all these announcements for things that are already over. I pay for them myself. There are no editions; there is just the archive edition. In advertising you send out 200 posters and hope that 20 people come to the event. When you do it after the fact, you just make the 20 and give it to people who actually came to the event." Fella's experimental graphics give him an opportunity to create work associated with events but that do not advertise them ahead of time. They are graphic souvenirs and function to promote ideas rather than events, thus clearly reflecting the work and thought process of the designer.

Designer/Illustrator: Ed Fella

FELLA,

PRESENT IN AN ART DESIGNERIST TYPE SLIDE PRESENTATION

AT YALE UNIVERSITY
8 pm graphic design
TUESDAY 27th PROGRAM,
NOVEMBER SCHOOL OF ART

13-24
Working with Clients

Graphic design is, on the whole, a client-driven art form. The presence of a client is what often, but not always, distinguishes graphic design from "art" per se. Designers' relationships with clients vary so greatly that it is difficult to make generalizations about how exactly to deal with this necessary element. For example, a large firm like Wieden+Kennedy has a very different approach to clients than a small studio like Why Not Associates with three or four employees. If your company has an accounts department that is responsible for strategic relations, designers can potentially have little to do with the client, outside of idea meetings and presentations. On the other hand, the designer in a small studio or firm may have to be the account manager, director of new business development, accounts payable officer, and strategic planner—in addition to coming up with and executing the brilliant, original ideas. Complicating this category even further is the fact that clients come in all shapes and sizes, from large, multitiered corporations to small, nonprofit organizations. Projects can range from complete identity system development to a single brochure.

In this chapter, we present widely diverse advice on client interaction from designers. We provide an overview of the context in which these interactions take place and describe how designers have handled difficult situations, large and small. In addition, some of the designers we talked to don't actually have clients but are graphic designers who pursue their work through other means. These voices provide insight about the role of the client in the creative process and describe the creative models by which some designers pursue their art. By showing some of the many variables that govern the designer-client relationship, we demonstrate some of the best practices in this relationship and some strategies for maintaining and nurturing this relationship.

⑬ Visit the client's site—physical and virtual

Zumtobel annual report
Stefan Sagmeister

In completing their first annual report, Sagmeister Studio discovered that the process differed from less conventional jobs such as music packaging. The client was Zumtobel, a European manufacturer. Sagmeister flew to the Zumtobel headquarters to immerse himself in their business. They gave him an extensive tour of their factory, showing him what they had done in the past and where they were in the present. Sagmeister returned to New York and worked out one very tight suggestion for the annual report based on what he learned about their business on his visit. They liked what they saw and adopted the design.

Sagmeister had sensed immediately that the client was unusual. He met with the CEO, who said that there was a 95 percent chance that the design, whatever it might be, would be adopted without reservation. This was a singular occasion for Sagmeister, who at first thought it was somewhat foolish of the CEO to reveal such information. "I could have just as easily taken advantage of it and come back with three half-penises on the cover. But as it happens in real life, if you get a lot of trust, you are very unlikely to misuse it," he comments.

Sagmeister believes this trust was established because of his face-to-face interaction with the CEO and the physical interaction with the space of the company. He knew for himself that he could not submit a design without being 100 percent happy with it. With this design, however, he was convinced of its appropriateness to the project at hand and knew that it fit the client's needs exactly. He notes, "The fact that we pushed it to that point had a lot to do with the trust we established because of a meeting."

Designer: Stefan Sagmeister

THE
METROPOLITAN
OPERA

⑭ Research client decision-making systems

Metropolitan Opera re-identitification
Worldstudio, Inc.

Worldstudio, Inc., undertook a large identity project for the
Metropolitan Opera, which involved navigating an extremely
complex bureaucracy. The Metropolitan Opera hired
Worldstudio because the new development director recognized
that they needed to solve some important identity issues at
the organization, which had a less-than-consistent identity.
For example, new hires at the Metropolitan Opera had to
design their own business cards. As a result, everybody had
their own business cards, all with different logos, different
wording, and different looks. The inconsistency made the
development director's job difficult because the organization
appeared to be so fragmented.

The development director went to the executive director and
convinced him that they needed to hire a studio to get the
identity materials in order. Each department of the Met is highly
politicized, according to Mark Randall from Worldstudio, so they
all—from publicity to promotions to design to scenics—were
simply doing things the way they always had, and the Met was

successful. Worldstudio, Inc., came to discover that this entrenchment would be the major challenge of the job.

Worldstudio decided the only way to get anything done was to get people on board with the idea of change and to give them some ownership in the process. They interviewed all 13 department heads, talking to each person for over an hour. The department heads told Worldstudio what they thought the strengths of the Met were and what they wanted to communicate. The result was an "Objectives and Strategies" statement, which was circulated to and signed off by those same people. In this way, Worldstudio had a platform with the client on which to base the project.

The Worldstudio designers then worked with another group of six department heads and the general manager, meeting to discuss all the key points of the identity development. It was probably the most client-involved process the studio had ever done, and it took almost nine months to work through it.

Through the careful process of learning about the Metropolitan Opera, Worldstudio, Inc., was able to gain insight about a large, nonprofit client, which set them in a better position to pitch to such clients in the future. In addition, they learned about some of the pitfalls of working with an organization with so many departmental arms—as well as how to negotiate alliances and find support on many levels. They also learned that they should remain in the role of the designer and not to try to overhaul the system of an organization.

Designers: Mark Randall, David Sterling

⑮ Spend time with your client to build consensus and create shared goals

Sapporo Beer Dome
John C Jay, Weiden+Kennedy, Tokyo

A good fit between the goals of a client and the goals of a designer or design firm can be created in many ways. In his office in Tokyo, John C Jay cites this extensive getting-to-know-you practice as essential for his business. "We spend a lot of time learning about the client. We visit each other, talk, and take time to understand the client's culture, giving them time to understand ours."

A primary concern for Jay is developing the consensus-building process, as well as developing the trust of his client. He has had an additional hurdle of cross-cultural communication, an issue more and more designers face as international firms and corporations become the norm. Jay notes that the Japanese businesses with which he has worked are used to working with Japanese companies, presenting something of a stumbling block: "The big question [asked by Japanese companies] is 'How could you know us? How could pretend to know us?'"

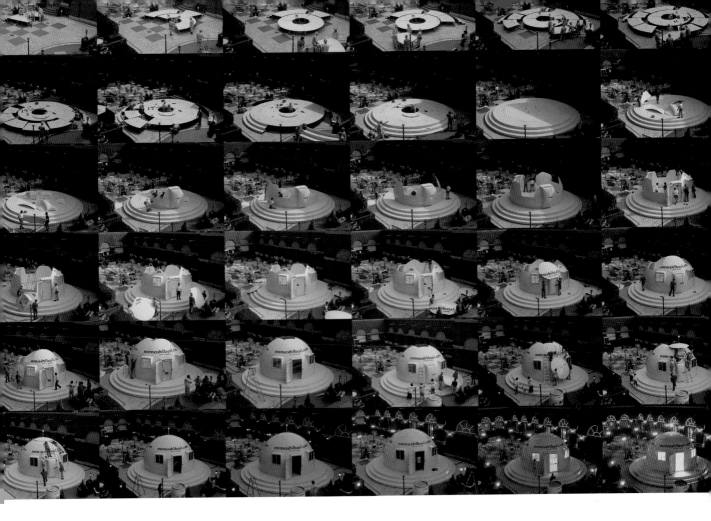

Jay cites building trust as foremost in this cross-cultural communication. Primarily staffed with Japanese designers, Wieden+Kennedy, Tokyo offers a blend, a hybrid of cultures. "We have the people who have the right DNA from a cultural standpoint, but they also have the right creative DNA. We just have to answer their questions and prove that we do understand them. That comes through a long series of discussions."

How and why would a Japanese company take a risk with a foreign company? Jay comments, "There are people who gravitate toward us, who already know something about us because of our work for Nike. As we began carving out a niche for ourselves and creating top Japanese brands, the walls came down. The proof is in our work and how successfully we can build projects piece by piece. If the question is, is it difficult to find people who share our passion for creativity, sure, it's hard. It's hard all over the world. But they are there; you just have to sort through

the mess. Once you start sharing a business relationship, it is vitally important that a partnership is struck. Our goal is to earn their trust, and trust is not built through some presentation. Trust is built one meeting at a time, one campaign at a time, one project at a time. Hopefully there is an intuition up front, and hopefully we can prove them right, and hopefully our intuition about them is right."

Creative Directors: John C Jay, Sumiko Sato
Art Director: Hiroshi Yonemura
Copywriters: Sumiko Sato, Kenji Enomoto
Production Coorindator: Doors

⑯ Expand your audience by doing public art projects

The Cursing Stone
Why Not Associates

The Cursing Stone and Reiver Pavement, which lists all the Reiver families from the area, is situated in the Tullie House Museum and Art Gallery in the northwestern English town of Carlisle. A collaboration with artist Gordon Young, the Cursing Stone is a 7.5-ton (6,804 kg) granite boulder inscribed with a 16th-century curse issued by the archbishop of Glasgow upon the Anglo-Scottish Reiver families who terrorized the borderlands at that time. The curse is long, detailed, and harsh. Young had been commissioned to create a piece of art for an underground walkway at the museum, and because he was from the border-town where the curse was issued, he wanted to reproduce it somehow. His first inclination was to create a metal sphere, but he soon decided granite would be a more malleable medium.

In collaboration with Why Not, Young and the design team decided the curse should go around the sphere, which was a more difficult task than it initally appeared. Starting with a 9-ton (8,165 kg) boulder, Young eventually chipped and smoothed it down to a brilliant, smooth sheen. The text was applied as a mask and took three days to complete. It was then sand-blasted, leaving the curse on the stone.

Hundreds of people walk across the Reiver Pavement and look at the Cursing Stone each year. In addition, when it was initially completed, it garnered major media attention, and various local calamities, such as the recurrence of foot and mouth disease, were blamed on the resurrection of the curse. Collaborating with a fine artist to make a type-based sculpture allowed Why Not to gain access to an otherwise inaccessible audience.

Art Directors, Designers: Gordon Young, Why Not Associates
Photography: Rocco Redondo
Client: Carlisle City Council

⑰ Don't talk about CD art in a CD art meeting

OK Go CD packaging
Stefan Sagmeister

Stefan Sagmeister has developed an approach to music packaging that works. In general, he tries to talk to the band and to nobody else. This method is partially the result of a past trend in which when he found himself with three clients instead of one—the management, the label, and the band. Because that arrangement created problems for all three parties, Sagmeister tries to communicate with only one party, the most important one.

Sagmeister admits that he is lucky because the bands that come to him are interested in their packaging. Most of them have either rebelled against the label's in-house designers, or the in-house designers are just too busy to take on the band's project. In early meetings, Sagmeister keeps the subject off the art itself, talking instead about the music, the lyrics—where they came from, how they were written, why they were written—what the band thinks about the album. Next, Sagmeister gets rough cuts of the music to listen to as he designs. Finally, he comes back to the band with a recommendation, usually only one design that

he develops to look like the final piece. "Meeting with the band is the most important part," Sagmeister says. "By talking about the ideas of the music, as opposed to the band's ideas about art, we are more likely to come up with a good solution."

Designer: Stefan Sagmeister

MARC JACOBS

MARC JACOBS

⑱ All work has its own unique client

Marc Jacobs print advertising
Miles Murray Sorrell FUEL

Miles Murray Sorrell FUEL has worked with photographer Jürgen Teller for a number years, designing his books and exhibitions. This collaboration bore fruit when Teller was asked to shoot the campaign for the Marc Jacobs 2002 line. Although Miles Murray Sorrell FUEL discussed the ideas for the campaign with Teller, they did not direct him on his shoots. Their work for Jacobs includes advertising for clothes, shoes, bags, and perfume. The Marc Jacobs perfume campaign with Sofia Coppola won a Council of Fashion Designers of America Award.

Once Teller's photos were in, Miles Murray Sorrell FUEL worked with Teller to edit the photos. They then did the layouts and produced the artwork for the various ads. The idea that all work has its own client is particularly important for fashion design, where the look developed by the photographer and the graphic designer must be both unique and serve the clothing designer's work.

Every designer deserves work that is truly unique. Designers must continually reinvent themselves and maintain an understanding of the client and their needs. Only then can an appropriate solution be delivered.

Designers: Miles Murray Sorrell FUEL
Photography: Jürgen Teller

⑲ Learn the language of the client

Miller High Life: "Mayonnaise"
Todd Waterbury, Wieden+Kennedy, New York

The designer must create consistent language and messaging for a campaign to be successful. The designer must listen, learn, and adapt the language he or she hears from the client. In this manner, the creative ideas of the designer can effectively move from the design table and into the boardroom.

Because Todd Waterbury and the creative teams at Wieden+Kennedy have a particularly intuitive way of working, they cannot work with just any client. Waterbury calls the initial meeting with the client the "chemistry" meeting. It is here that the representatives from the firm discuss their philosophy of creative work and show their portfolio of recent campaigns. This is also when the clients describe their needs for the specific project, as well as overarching ideas about doing business and the client firm's core beliefs.

"Usually, once we show our work and talk about why we do what we do and how we believe in it, we can tell whether it is going to be a good fit," Waterbury notes. But there have also been times when his team has worked with a client in an effort to develop a dynamic and creative relationship over time. In some instances this has worked, and in others it hasn't. Companies who view business itself as a creative endeavor are generally more amenable to Wieden+Kennedy's approach than are companies who work within a strict paradigm of business practice.

Still, Waterbury notes that a dynamic and open environment can sometimes be the work of a single person within a corporate structure. "Even though the category or the industry may be seen by us, and by most people, as boring or dry, with the right people in the company who want to do something new, anything is possible. I genuinely believe that." In the initial meeting, Waterbury tries to keep an open mind to the opportunities that a company can offer his creative teams' and makes contact with the people within the client's company who he senses will be able to get things done.

Art Director: Jeff Williams
Copywriter: Jeff Kling
Producers: Jeff Selis, Tieneke Pavesic
Creative Directors: Dan Wieden, Susan Hoffman
Client: Miller High Life

"Mayonnaise" :15
VO: It's hard to respect the French when you have to
bail 'em out of two big ones in one century. But we
have to hand it to 'em on mayonnaise. Nice job Pierre.

Teach the client your language

ESPN Without Sports campaign
Todd Waterbury, Wieden+Kennedy, New York

Too often a creative person appeals to the client on the level of beauty, execution, or aesthetic cleverness, but he or she does not explain to the client how the idea will help them drive business.

The contrast between a small studio like Sagmeister's and a large advertising firm can shed light on the differences in approach that designers take to client interaction. In his work with Wieden+Kennedy, Todd Waterbury often works for large clients with complex decision-making and communication hierarchies. In most cases, the marketing director, the CEO, the COO, and the communications person are different people. Waterbury notes that creative people rarely translate their needs and desires accurately from language that they have grown up with into language that is articulate and meaningful to the client. When presenting ideas, the creative person needs to communicate with the client in such a way that the person he or she is talking to has a high level of clarity and conviction about what the idea is. In addition, and perhaps more importantly, the client needs to be given tools to sell the idea with a similar level of clarity and conviction back in the company where they work.

Waterbury reminds us that in the corporate model, marketing departments are cost centers, as opposed to revenue centers, and the client views money spent on marketing as an expense, investment that should yield returns. Every conversation with the client must involve language that incorporates this fundamental premise and uses it to create clear communication and conviction.

Waterbury has been working on a branding campaign for ESPN that is meant to reignite a connection to sports in the lapsed fan. The objective of the campaign is to move the meaning of sports off the gridiron or the court and remind people that sports influence everything from music and fashion to the whole celebrity machine. Waterbury conjoined all these disparate entities in the question, "What would the world be like without sports?", always bringing it back to the client's product: "Can you go without…ESPN?" Although the tag line was not used in the commercials, it was essential in conducting meetings with the client to keep bringing them back to the core message of the spots. In this way, the client could understand the central premise of the campaign and could communicate it clearly.

"Shelfball"
Creative Directors: Ty Montague, Todd Waterbury
Art Director: Kim Schoen
Copywriter: Kevin Proudfoot
Broadcast Producer: Brian Cooper
Production Company: RSA—Exec. Producer: Fran McGovern, Producer: Betina Schneider
Director: ACNE
Director of Photography: Jim Whitaker

"Coach"
Creative Directors: Ty Montague, Todd Waterbury
Art Director: Kim Schoen
Copywriter: Kevin Proudfoot
Broadcast Producer: Brian Cooper
Director: Stacy Wall
Director of Photography: Pieter Vermeer
Editor/Company: Stephane Dumonceau/Mad River Post
Music Composer/Company: Ray Loewy/Tonefarmer

"Teammates"
Creative Directors: Ty Montague, Todd Waterbury
Art Director: Kim Schoen
Copywriter: Kevin Proudfoot
Broadcast Producer: Brian Cooper
Production Company: 40 Acres & a mule—Producer: Butch Robinson
Director: Spike Lee
Director of Photography: Ellen Kuras
Editor/Company: Stephane Dumonceau/Mad River Post NY
Music Composer/Company: Brian Horton/Doc 8 Music

Client: ESPN

"Shelfball / Medical Condition" :30
VO 1: Homer! Yes, Yes.
VO 2: Nice, nice.
VO 3: It only bounced twice.
VO 1: No, no, I cleared it.
VO 2: So what? It's a home run.
VO 3: No, it's a double.
VO 1: No, it didn't even hit the back of the shelf.
VO 3: It bounces twice, it's a double.
VO 2: What are you talking about?
VO 3: I'm talking about rules—doesn't hit the back.
VO 1: Those aren't the rules. You're talking about making up the rules.
VO 3: No, I'm talking about… look, I play with shoes, you don't.
VO 1: So what?
VO 3: That's a rule.
VO 1: I have a medical condition.
VO 2: This is why no one wants to play with you.
VO 3: Why? Because I'm right, and I'm better at it than you?
VO 1: Take a nap.

"Coach" :60
VO1: We're still in it. Let's do it.
VO 2: Look at the game. Watch who got the ball, watch who got the ball.
VO 3: Now, that is mad-dog defense. That's a good defense. If they just work it a little, more like that.
VO 4: Impossible.
VO 5: Here we go.
VO 6: Nice tip, nice tip. Way to crash the board.
VO 7: Basketball 101, basketball 101.
VO 8: They need to hurry up. What are they taking their time for?
VO 2: Tackle somebody. Tackle somebody now!
VO 3: That's bush league. That's all it is. Nothing but bush league.
VO 6: Fourth quarter they always collapse.
VO 9: Push it, Fisher.
VO 11: Come on!
VO 12: Terry's open, he's open, he's open!
VO 1: Run, baby, run. Run.
VO 11: Knock him down!
VO 4: Don't foul.
VO 12: Foul him!
VO 13: Let it go!
VO 4: What did I say?
VO 1: Beautiful.
VO 2: Make a play.
VO 3: Hit him for God's sake.
VO 11: Run it left. Run it left!
VO 2: No, just him, somebody.
VO 3: Take him on the boards.
VO 1: Go, baby, go!
VO 3: It's a disgrace, just a disgrace. They ought to be ashamed of themselves.
VO 1: Now, that's what I'm talking about!

"Teammates" :60
VO 1: May 13, 1947, we were playing in Crossly field.
VO 2: The fans in Cincinnati were not very pro-black baseball player at that time.
VO 3: Now, even though it's in the north, north of the Ohio River, it basically was a southern town in their thinking.
VO 2: It was like going into a morass of discrimination, that's what it was…it was discrimination, segregation.
VO 3: The fans were all over Jackie, giving him verbal abuse…and a…and some of them were very rank.
VO 1: They were ruckus and were on Jackie's case, I mean, they were saying anything they could about Jackie, all the racial slurs they could conceive.
VO 2: And Peewee Reese, a white baseball player with the Dodgers from Louisville, Kentucky, came over to second base.
VO 3: And put his arm around him.
VO 1: Put his arm around his shoulder.
VO 2: And put his arm around Jackie Robinson, a black man with the Dodgers from Cairo, Georgia.

(21) Seek out creative clients for successful collaborations

Kama Sutra packaging
Margo Chase, Chase Design Group

The Chase Design Group has been working with the Kama Sutra company for eight years. The company was founded and is owned by Joe Bolstad, who himself has a degree in design. "He's the only client I've ever had who graduated from Art Center," comments Margo Chase. "I think his degree in design is part of the reason we've been able to do such a good job with his products."

When Bolstad came to the Chase Design Group, the packaging for his products had been the same since 1965. The products were sold primarily in head shops and sex stores, but Bolstad wanted to grow the business and get his products into larger gift shops and department stores.

"The Kama Sutra name was our inspiration," says Chase. "We researched the original Indian artwork, paintings, and frescos and presented several different ideas for how to incorporate that feeling into their packaging. In the end, we created two different looks. The core product line, which includes Oil of Love, Pleasure Balm, and Honey Dust, is wrapped in a green, ribbed

paper with a gold metallic leaf pattern. Each flavor has a different bellyband design to distinguish it and tie it into the gift product line, which is decorated with illustrations based on the art of the original Kama Sutra."

Because of the redesign, Kama Sutra products can now be found in high-end gift stores all over the world, as well as at mainstream retailers like Long's Drug. Their business has grown every year since Chase Design Group has worked with them—their sales doubled in 2002 alone. Close collaboration with the company's owner elevated the dialog about developing designs to a very sophisticated level, creating an exciting and ultimately successful partnership.

Art Director: Margo Chase
Designers: Jonathan Sample, Patricia Guerra
Illustrator: Marilee Heyer
Studio: Chase Design Group
Client: The Kama Sutra Company

㉒ Build small projects into engaging, ongoing work

Gilbert Paper promotions
Worksight

A small project for Gilbert Paper ended up turning into a series on American subcultures for Worksight. "I found a culture at the paper company and that turned into other paper promos for other American subcultures, such as Coney Island, sturgeon spearing on Lake Winnebago, and a piece about Jackson Hole, Wyoming, called 'Branding the Great American West,'" says Scott Santoro of Worksight. Santoro asked the company if he could explore these subcultures in the context of a paper promotion, and they agreed. "Why do these cultures exist? What is so cool about them? Why would we want to tell their story? What do we find embedded in them that would be interesting to talk about? It all started from this one piece that we did on their hundred-year-old paper mill."

In developing a promotion for a paper company, the designer must show the capacity of the product and demonstrate its most salient characteristics. But this is virtually the only requirement, and paper companies often give creative license to designers when creating promotions. "They wanted me to make up my

own assignment and turn it into a series," comments Santoro. "They wanted me to find tactile, textured stories that were interesting to me and then print them on their tactile, textured paper in the form of brochures that might interest other designers as well." By choosing to focus his work on subculture forms and figures such as cowboys, Santoro created projects that were definitely outside the mainstream, yet were useful for the paper company to show off their product.

Designer: Scott Santoro/Worksight
Photography: Lon Murdick
Copywriter: Augustine Hope

㉓ Work for the government

Queen Elizabeth II stamps
Why Not Associates

"Working for the queen was probably the strangest job we've ever done," comments Andy Altmann of Why Not. In designing a series of postage stamps featuring the visage of Queen Elizabeth II, Why Not ran into many new and interesting issues about designing in a public context and for a public agency.

"The queen obviously has a lot attached to her. You want to do something your mother will like, and, at the same time, you want to do something contemporary. You can't make it too kitsch, but you are trying to tell a story over five stamps. It isn't easy." One of three design groups that were asked to come up with ideas for a new stamp, Why Not was successful on their first bid. In addition, the process of working for the Royal Mail lacked the bureaucracy that attends even some small private firms who hire designers. They did have to run their final proposals by the queen, who gave her assent.

Art Directors, Designers: Why Not Associates
Photography: Cecil Beaton, Anwar Hussein, Tim Graham
Client: Royal Mail

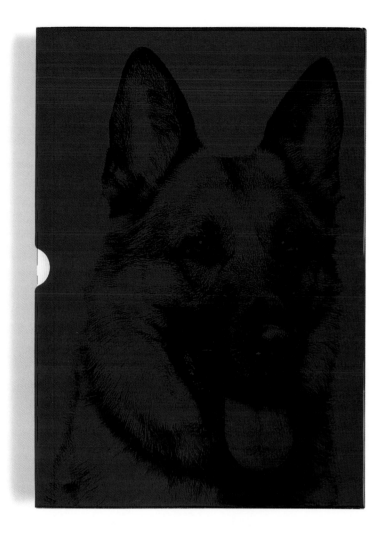

㉔ Develop a clear ethic of client
interaction that works for you

Made You Look
Stefan Sagmeister

In determining how to approach a client, many designers try to understand the organization of the client structure and go from there. Before this even happens, Stefan Sagmeister asks a series of questions that helps him make decisions about which clients to work for. Although the answers to these questions are highly subjective, their general structure may be useful to other designers as they make choices about who to work for.

Sagmeistster asks the following questions: How good is the product? How worthwhile are the client's activities? How much does he like the person who will be his daily contact? Do they have the money and the time to do the job properly? And is it challenging and exciting, or something we have done before?

Every choice that a designer makes about his or her business is rooted in his or her own ethical code. Developing and sustaining such a code is essential to making good and consistent choices about work.

Designer: Stefan Sagmiester

3

Workflow and In-House Dynamics

Getting the job done in the most effective way is the designer's goal in any client-driven context. Because the designers we talked to provided descriptions of such a wide range of work environments, generalizations were difficult to make and advice was sometimes contradictory. Each case study, however, provides a different facet of the real work processes and shows how a variety of problems were overcome. Ideas about the delegation of responsibility can range from specific employee assignments to group discussion on each major aspect of the project. This chapter makes suggestions about the best ways to work for yourself and with your colleagues when executing any given project in an effective and timely manner.

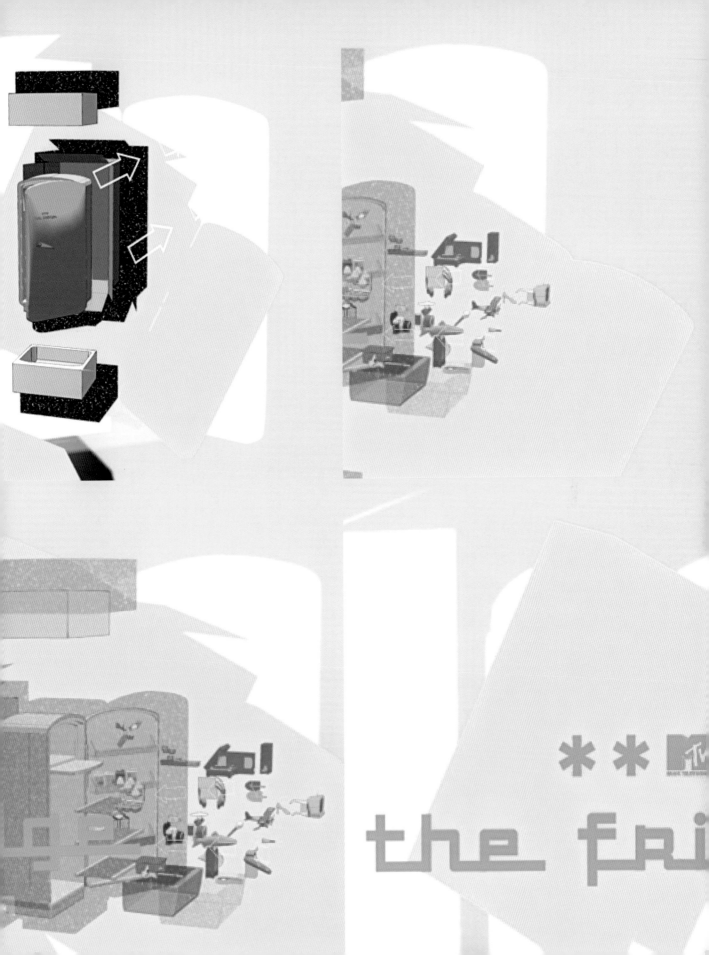

** MTV

the fri

LANDON DONOVAN WEARS NIKE SPHERE TECHNOLOGY

²⁵ Find an emotional connection with your audience

Nike Apparel print ads
Todd Waterbury, Wieden+Kennedy, New York

Whereas some agencies spend a lot of time and money testing their advertising—addressing it with a scientific model of effectiveness—Waterbury stresses the importance of finding the emotional connection and inspiration in the audiences he speaks to. The scientific method quantifies data, which is only useful for analyzing events of the past. It does not predict the future, and it does not set trends. Because Wieden+Kennedy place a premium on the cultural relevancy of their campaigns, only a forward-looking model can power the organization.

When some clients look at the Wieden+Kennedy portfolio, they wonder if their product or service can match the "fun" and "exciting" nature of clients like Nike, ESPN, or Miller. "We have to remind them that the category wasn't so exciting before we came in. If you look at the sneaker category in 1971, it wasn't even a developed category. If you look at the cheap beer category before we got into it, I mean, who wants to advertise cheap beer? That blue-collar thing was probably the most

rejected idea you could think of," Todd Waterbury notes. By
working with the client to communicate the potential of the
product or service and to show and describe the creative
strengths of the Wieden+Kennedy teams, Waterbury feels he
can help companies take risks they might not otherwise want to
take. "At the end of the day, the success of a project relies on
people, not on companies," he says.

Waterbury and his teams seek out people within the corporate
structures of the companies they work for, identifying those
who make up what he calls the "microworlds" of the company
culture. People who are changing the landscape or taking a
risk are the people with whom Waterbury wants to work. If they
end up moving from one job or industry to another, Waterbury
follows them, because he knows that they will be able to offer
a potential openness and influence as they shift from place
to place.

Art Director: Storm Tharp
Copywriter: Jonathan Cude
Creative Director: Todd Waterbury
Studio Artist: Jan Meyer
Photographer: Liz Collins
Client: Nike

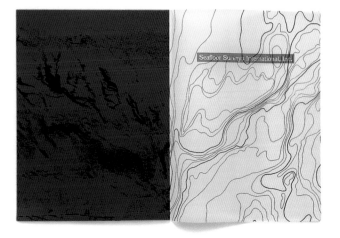

㉖ Demand respect, creative license, and fair pay

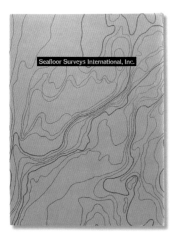

Budweiser advertising, Seafloor International brochure
Art Chantry

Art Chantry observes, "Graphic design is a weird art form; it is half business, half art. Most people who get into it do so because of the art. The successful ones get into it for the business. You may be a critical success doing art, but you are not going to get rich."

In making ethical choices about who to work for and what kind of jobs to take, Chantry decided that the system is designed to "make hypocrites out of all of us." In his early career, he was not particularly picky about who he worked for, recognizing the parallels between small and large businesses, even when one purported to be "independent" or "alternative." Chantry found working for corporations to be extremely difficult, because he perceived that decisions were made out of fear and within an extremely complex hierarchy. Often the nebulous "legal department" was called in to finalize choices about art—something Chantry finds antithetical to the process of making a good design. In addition, the process of actually getting paid by corporations was arduous and protracted.

At a certain point in the late '80s, Chantry decided to be more discriminating about his clients, and, as he puts it, "not work for assholes anymore." Instead of a few big jobs, he did a lot of small jobs and was suddenly overwhelmed with work instead of having to search it out.

Now when he assesses new clients, he uses what he calls the "bullshit meter," which is a measure of fakery and manipulation from the client's end. He is not willing to work in an environment where he is not respected, given creative license, or paid fairly for his work.

In Chantry's view, the graphic design business suffers from a delusion that it is somehow morally superior to the advertising industry because of its closer affiliation with "art." However, it is advertising's self-proclaimed mission to make money and, exploit images for the purpose of selling products. Graphic design, as a colluding agent in this process, should come clean about its own culpability.

Chantry admits, "Sometimes I actually will do work for clients I don't like simply because I really believe in the project. I've turned down some huge-monied clients because I thought they sucked as institutions or as projects or even as personalities. However, I'm not suicidal—if they threw *enough* money at me, I'd certainly say yes. Then I'd turn around and use that money to help finance my work for clients I believe in. We're all whores, ya know."

Designer: Art Chantry

Expand with your clients

Esolis Launch materials
Worldstudio, Inc.

Worldstudio, Inc., did a project for the launch of a new skin care company called Esolis. In working with this client, they were able to use many of the skills they had already developed from working with other cosmetics clients. The nature of this job forced them to develop new skills and take on new challenges as their work with the client expanded.

Initially, Worldstudio developed the naming for the company and designed its market launch materials. This particular line of cosmetics was targeted toward Asian American women, and research told them that these women tend to do a lot of catalog and online shopping. Developing an attractive and useful Web site was a priority for the client, particularly one that showcased the technological aspect of the product that they were selling. Instead of the more familiar style of cosmetics advertisement, Worldstudio had to work to manipulate a lot of information about the various products into an easily navigable

and aesthetically clean form. The scientific basis of the Esolis product became the foundation for the Web site as well as for the catalog materials.

As the project grew and the product line increased, Worldstudio, Inc., was asked to handle all of the product and model photography for both the Web site and the catalog. Because Esolis was growing organically, the process and methods that the studio employed had to reflect and complement that growth. What started as a naming project soon developed into a much larger assignment, and the initial assignment soon expanded into a diverse range of projects and an ongoing relationship with the client.

Art Directors: David Sterling, Tom Koken
Designer: Daniela Koenn
Photographers: Torkil Gundnason, Rick Burda
Client: Esolis

VO: Leather seats, automatic transmission. Nowadays you'll hear people call this a truck. Well, a man knows a station wagon when he sees one. This car will only see off-road action if someone backs over a flower bed. If this vehicular masquerade represents the high life to which men are called, we should trade our trousers for skirts right now.

㉘ Develop brands that both reflect and influence culture

Miller High Life: "SUV"
Todd Waterbury, Wieden+Kennedy, New York

In contrast to the small studio of Worldstudio, Inc., Todd Waterbury directs a team of creative people at the New York office of Wieden+Kennedy. The work he does there ranges from television commercials to print ads to identity work and packaging, as well as everything that serves to communicate what a brand stands for. The firm is the global agency for Nike and ESPN and is now working with Avon to develop a new generation of products for teens. This year Nike was awarded the prestigious Golden Lion award at Cannes for their comprehensive global advertising campaign—an award that in turn bestows accolades on the work of Wieden+Kennedy.

For each of these clients, however, Waterbury has an overarching philosophy: the way that brands influence people's lives extends beyond traditional media, and people need to be able to embrace the brand at more intimate and respected levels than simply passively viewing a commercial on TV or in a magazine. This tall order involves a process that purveys to the audience an emotional connection to the brand and places it in the general suffusion of culture over a variety of human experiences.

Art Director: Jeff Williams
Copywriter: Jeff Kling
Producers: Jeff Selis, Tieneke Pavesic
Creative Directors: Dan Wieden, Susan Hoffman

SAVE FUEL

Help save electricity

Save Fuel poster
Miles Murray Sorrell FUEL

Although somewhat obvious, Miles Murray Sorrell FUEL insists that one of its mantras of work is to always be open to new ideas. The "Save Miles Murray Sorrell FUEL" poster was designed in 1992 as part of a series for Virgin Records. It was one of Miles Murray Sorrell FUEL's first commissions as a group and was screen-printed by them at the Royal College of Art. Playing on the name of their group, they were able to convey a relatively uncontroversial ecological sentiment.

This sentiment may be important to the people involved at FUEL because they went to school together. The idea of collaborating under one light and gathering in the common room resonates with a sense of mutual purpose and interdependence.

Designer: Miles Murray Sorrell FUEL

③⓪ If you are a designer, design; if you are a manager, manage

Made You Look spreads
Stefan Sagmeister

The flow of work through Sagmeister Studio is not complex. Initially, it comes in through Stefan Sagmeister. He works on it with his designer, Mattias Erstberger, and then it goes out through Sagmeister. Having only two designers in the office naturally limits the volume of work. At times, there are interns who Sagmeister judges to be particularly talented, and they work on jobs, too. Sagmeister takes on interns only if they are able to commit full-time to the studio—this generally means the person cannot have another job in addition to his or her work at the studio.

This pared-down office is a conscious choice for Sagmeister, whose previous work experiences reflected a very different model. When Sagmeister worked for Leo Burnett in Hong Kong, he had a much larger group of handpicked designers. In that context, he was more of a manager, and, from his perspective,

managing a small design group is among the least interesting jobs there is. "If I would want to become a manager, I would much rather go to business school and work on Wall Street where you actually have some challenges," he comments.

Sagmeister serves as the art director for all of the work that comes through the studio. Keeping the chain of command simplified, particularly if you are the commander, makes for an efficient and focused work environment.

Designer: Stefan Sagmeister

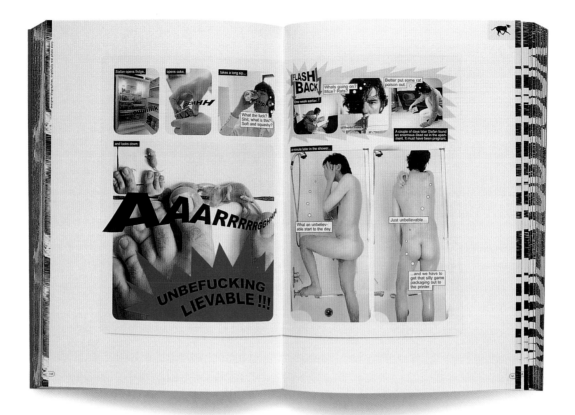

(31) # Accessible can be smart; smart can be funny

Eric Morecambe statue and grounds
Why Not Associates

Why Not Associates place a premium on sense of humor when approaching design problems. A fan of comedy himself, partner Andy Altmann was quite pleased when he was able to help with the Tern redevelopment project in Morecambe, near Lancaster. Rather than featuring a public servant in the classical sense, the redevelopment project proposed a statue of Eric Morecambe, the comedian who is closely associated with the town of Morecambe. By selecting a figure that melded with local culture and history, the designers were able to dispute the idea that only generals and princes could be the subject of statues, but that a man who made people laugh was worthy of commemoration.

In collaboration with artist Gordon Young and sculptor Russell Coleman, Why Not Associates surrounded the statue of the comedian with quotes from some of his better-known sketches.

Client: Lancaster City Council
Art Direction, Designers: Gordon Young, Why Not Associates
Photography: Jerry Hardman Jones

㉜ Hire interesting, creative people— and listen to them

Pony skin shoes
John C Jay, Wieden+Kennedy, Tokyo

One of the most important parts of John C Jay's creative direction is establishing a vision for the office. Jay consistently asks: Who do you hire? How do you maintain the most interesting and skilled people in your company? He notes, "I want to bring in the most skilled, of course, but I also want the most interesting people who lead the most interesting lives–people who bring something into the office besides just focusing on a typeface."

If you go to the fourth floor of Wieden+Kennedy's office in Tokyo, you will find a studio full of DJ equipment-mixers and turntables so that employees can work on their music. This kind of accommodation was part of the Tokyo office when it was founded in 1998. Jay notes, "It all started with asking, what kind of people are interesting to have around you? The idea that an agency would need 'cool hunters' or researchers is just kind of proof that you don't know what is going on."

Wieden+Kennedy, Tokyo has two DJs on staff, including one whose DJ career competes with his ad agency career. How does a company support these creative people? "We give them outlets. They are also on salary, of course. One wanted time off to go to the Barcelona Music Festival, for example, so he went. We support music people in our company in a variety of ways. And we ask them to produce events with us."

One such event was the Tokyo Designers Block, in which Wieden+Kennedy teamed up with a company called Sputnik and Kurisaki (who is known as the Japanese "dean of design"). Together, they created an exhibit, which involved taking over a planetarium in the middle of Shibuya, turning it into a celebration of 1970s design in Japan, specifically the Osaka Expo. The VJs and DJs who worked for Wieden+Kennedy created an experience inside the dome in which images were projected inside the entire planetarium. These kinds of project are only possible with the right teams in-house to develop and drive them.

Another example of the unique approach to staff composition is an exclusive shoe design made for Wieden+Kennedy, Tokyo. The shoes were a limited edition of the Nike Air Force One. Designed by Hiroshi Fujiwara, they were made by Nike in celebration of the opening of the new Wieden+Kennedy office in Tokyo. The pony skin sneaker was for staff only. The typography on back of the shoe, designed by the studio, spells "Tokyo." Inside the tongues are special Wieden+Kennedy Tokyo labels along with the special silver tips on the laces. These shoes were never for sale to the general public.

Creative Directors: John C Jay, Hiroshi Fujiwara

CONSID R
TH
H IS NB RG
UN RTAINTY
PRIN IPL

AND I KNOW
WHERE I'M GOING,

IMPOSSIBLE

ACTIVITY

(33) Always keep the valve
in the open position

Sci-Fi Channel ID tags
Miles Murray Sorrell FUEL

These words and images are taken from one of a series of
animated identities that Miles Murray Sorrell FUEL produced
for the Sci-Fi Channel. The Sci-Fi brief was flexible, but the
main idea for the campaign was to produce something
with a philosophical and scientific feel that challenged any
audience preconception that the network solely caters to
traditional science-fiction enthusiasts.

FUEL came up with the idea of a sinister voice, something
between a warning and an advertisement. They chose the
topics in the identities because either they are fundamental to
science fiction or they have some relevance to the audience.
They are intentionally phrased so that the viewer is left
questioning the topic's validity.

Staying open to what ideas and images were related to the
broader category of science fiction made it possible for FUEL to
develop a creative and flexible campaign for a client who was

trying to expand their market—and, hence, the meaning—of
their product. In a larger sense, this approach means considering intellectual and aesthetic ideas that may not be initially
attractive or even useful. To do this, a designer must be not only
a good researcher, but an active cultural participant as well.

Designers: Miles Murray Sorrell FUEL

㉞ Cultivate a workplace with a specific look and sound

Chase Design Group studio space
Margo Chase, Chase Design Group

In Margo Chase's office, she cultivates an air of excited calm. "I'm lucky, because Chase Design Group is a lively place filled with talented people and not a lot of ego issues. Conversation and open exchange of ideas flow freely. Even in the creative group, when a project is being executed by one designer it often gets kicked around, and the ideas get better. One of the things I look for when I hire designers is people who are open to that and not threatened by it."

What makes the studio unique? "Really loud music! We have an open plan in the creative department, and lots of conversations happen with everyone. We all have a great rapport, and we discuss all kinds of things, from politics to design, as a group. For some reason the business people upstairs prefer it quieter."

The design of the office serves the hierarchy of decision making at the Design Group. "There are three executives who make the important decisions: myself (as creative director), Chris Lowery

(minister of the environment and production manager), and James Bradley (president). Sometimes we all agree, which makes things easy, but there's often a lot of conflict between us that we have to talk through. This leads to better decisions. James believes very strongly that a conflict-free business is the wrong goal. We embrace conflict as essential and a sign of life," adds Chase.

In addition to these decisions at the top, everyone in the office is encouraged to express his or her opinions about each project. Chase notes, "Even a bad or stupid-sounding idea may trigger something great. As creative director, I spend a lot of my time talking to designers about the work they are doing to make sure that they are really thinking things through and looking at their solutions from every angle."

Photography: James Bradley

㉟ Keep decision making simple and nonhierarchical

The Fridge title sequence
Why Not Associates

Why Not Associates formed in part because the skills of three came in handier than the skills of one. Andy Altmann remembers, "The three of us were in college together, and we graduated in 1987, myself, David Ellis, and Howard Greenhalgh. [Greenhalgh] was asked to design a magazine, which he said he could do. He came up to the college and said, 'I've got to do a magazine. Can you help me?' Later, we thought up a name and set up a studio in Soho. Greenhalgh always wanted to do film things, so he eventually ended up doing pop videos. And we were doing graphics, so we were doing a mixture of things. Eventually he also set up Why Not Films to produce the pop videos, and we had two companies, Why Not Associates and Why Not Films. That was 15 years ago."

Why Not Associates is not a business that works in any traditional, hierarchical system. When a job comes in, it is usually fronted by one of the partners. He goes to meet the client, decides who is free or who is best suited to that particular project, and then works with the client and sorts out some ideas. One of the partners takes the lead, and the rest of the office collaborates on it. Some other jobs might be done by only one person. All the ideas get aired in the office, and everyone at Why Not gets a say in the project. "Is it any good? Does it make sense?" This process of sharing is a vital ingredient to the creative life of the office. "I couldn't work on my own," comments Altmann. "The client really wants just one point of contact, which makes it easier for them. Because we are so small, we know what is going on. I can just look over my Mac and see two other screens, I can see what is going on."

One example of this collaborative spirit guided by a singular vision is the graphics for the MTV Europe program, *The Fridge*. This show airs on Friday evenings and is meant to be watched while preparing for an evening on the town. Because the title of the show does not bear any particular relevance to the subject matter, when Why Not was selected to do the titling and opening sequence, there was not much direction in terms of the relationship between the word *fridge* and the idea of the show. Ellis came up with a diagrammatic style to treat the materials and worked within his office to see the project through to fruition.

Design and Art Direction: Why Not Associates
3D Animation: Peter Menich
Client: MTV Nordic and European

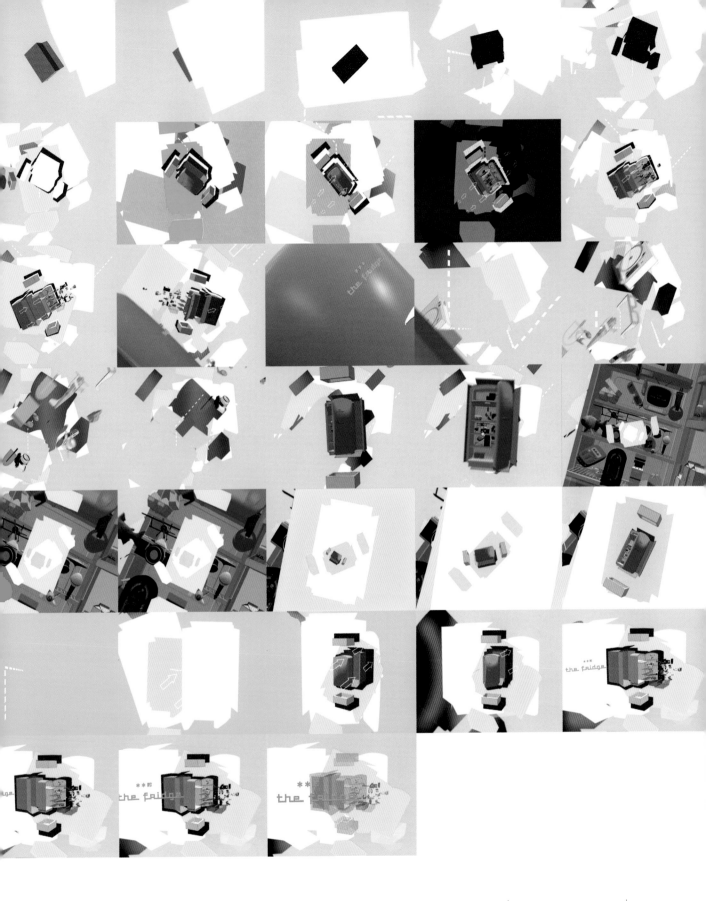

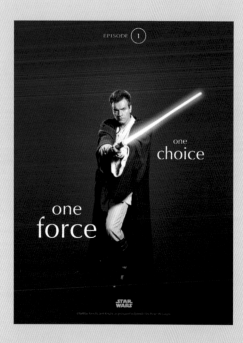

㊱ Creative directors need to stay creative

Star Wars, Episode One international ad campaign
John C Jay, Studio J

John C Jay does an amazing job of balancing the mangage-
ment of his award-winning creative team at Wieden+Kennedy,
Tokyo, and running his own freelance studio, Studio J. At this
studio he takes on jobs with high-profile clients such as
Lucasfilm, for which he did the Star Wars, Episode One advertising campaign for Asia and Europe. He comments, "Wieden+
Kennendy at this stage is a lot about creative mangement
responsibilities, but at the heart of my existence I'm still an art
director and designer. Certainly through my talented staff, I'm
able to implement some of my thinking."

In addition to doing design work, Jay also writes and researches,
developing his ideas for other media outside graphic design.
The most recent ideas he's worked with in the Presto campaign
for Nike came from an article he wrote for the American magazine SOMA about the importance of the post-wild-style grafitti
generation. "I wrote about how they were gathering in this tiny
town in Tokyo called Naka Meguro, which has become a mecca

for post-grafitti artists from all over the world, and how their art appears on lamp posts and walls and so forth, and how these people were completely different from the first grafitti artists. This article became kind of like a launching pad for that Presto idea. The influences can come through my writing. Currently I am working on a basketball project as an art director. I do a number of diverse projects."

Creative Director, Art Director: John C Jay/Studio J
Designers: Joshua Berger, Pete McCracken/Plazm, Markus Kiersztan/MP
Design Firm: Studio J
Client: Lucasfilm

㊲ Look far and wide for your sources in the creative process

Madonna "Drowned World" tour logo
Margo Chase, Chase Design Group

When developing the logo for pop star Madonna's "Drowned World" tour in 2001, Chase Design Group approached the work by gathering as much source information as possible. Doing the work to research and describe the aesthetic foundation of a particular design is essential to the way this company arrives at its final decisions.

Chase Design Group developed a custom icon and logo type to convey the unique and ethereal qualities of Madonna's show—described by Chase as "a multilayered musical and spiritual journey through diverse worlds"—as well as to address some of her personal interests. "Madonna is a student of the kabala, and she requested that we include references to that body of knowledge," comments Chase.

Chase's design references and incorporates both Arabic and Hebrew letterforms. In addition, the design references the mystical connections between religions and the idea of an intellectual as well as a physical journey. The design pictured was one of many logo designs that Chase proposed, but not the one that Madonna ultimately chose. "This one was my favorite because it referred to more specific aspects of her show and because I had the chance to create the new letterforms."

Art Director, Designer: Margo Chase
Client: Madonna

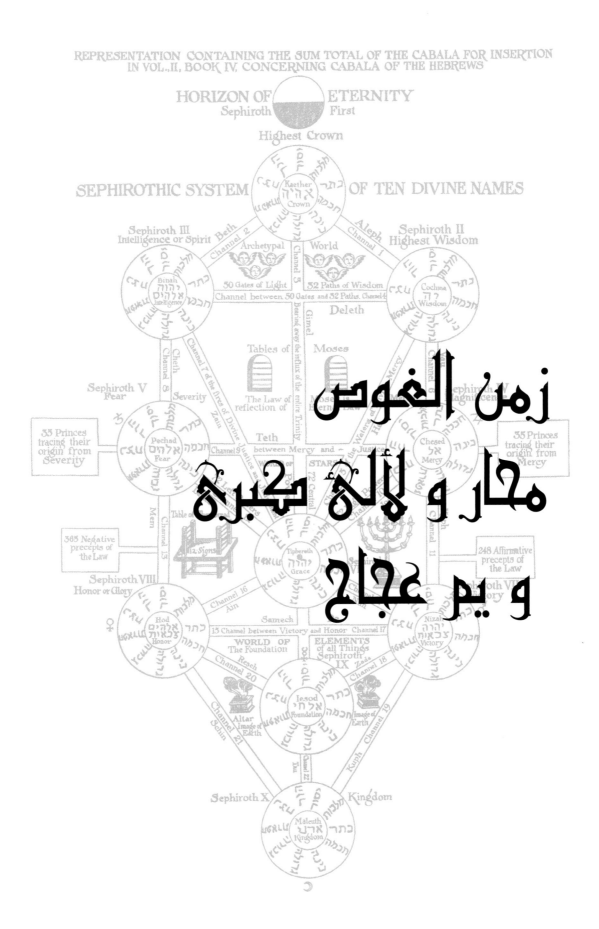

REPRESENTATION CONTAINING THE SUM TOTAL OF THE CABALA FOR INSERTION
IN VOL., II, BOOK IV, CONCERNING CABALA OF THE HEBREWS

HORIZON OF ETERNITY
Sephiroth First

Highest Crown

SEPHIROTHIC SYSTEM OF TEN DIVINE NAMES

Kaether
Crown

Sephiroth III
Intelligence or Spirit Beth Channel 2

Aleph Channel 1

Sephiroth II
Highest Wisdom

Archetypal World

Binah
Intelligence

50 Gates of Light

52 Paths of Wisdom

Cochma
Wisdom

Channel between, 50 Gates and 32 Paths, Channel 4

Deleth

Cheth Channel 8

Channel 7 of the fires of Divine Justice

Gimel

Tables of

Moses

Zain

The Law of reflection of

Sephiroth V
Fear

Severity

زمن الغوص

Sephiroth IV
Magnificence

Chesed
Mercy

35 Princes
tracing their
origin from
Severity

Pechad
Fear

Teth

Channel 9

between Mercy and Justice

محار و لألة مكبرة

35 Princes
tracing their
origin from
Mercy

STAR

Mem Channel 13

Table of 12 Signs

Tiphereth
Grace

و يم عجاج

365 Negative
precepts of
the Law

248 Affirmative
precepts of
the Law

Sephiroth VIII
Honor or Glory

Channel 16 Ain

Samech

Hod
Honor

15 Channel between Victory and Honor Channel 17

Nizah
Victory

WORLD OF
The Foundation

Resch Channel 20

ELEMENTS
of all Things
Sephiroth
IX Zade Channel 18

Altar
Image of
Earth

Iesod
Foundation

Image of
Earth

Channel 21 Schin

Kuph Channel 19

Channel 22 Tau

Sephiroth X

Kingdom

Maleuth
Kingdom

4

38-50
Continuing Education and
Professional Development

For this chapter, we interviewed designers about how they continue to educate themselves throughout the course of their careers. We wondered: What makes designers push themselves to new intellectual limits? What makes them think critically about their work and the practice of design? Does this searching have any tangible effect on design itself?

Stimulation from subjects and ideas outside one's own realm of expertise can spark new and creative ways of approaching a project. Whether it's going to a conference that does not have design as its focus or learning a new technique from a colleague, most of the designers we interviewed emphasize the importance of education outside the field of design as essential to their ongoing growth and expression as designers.

Tracing the direct results in the work of a designer who attends conferences and other educational forums that are not specifically about design is difficult. Nonetheless, it is a common theme among designers that getting the stimulus from fields outside of their own expertise has a direct and pronounced effect on the breadth and vitality of their work.

⊗ Avoid design conferences

AIGA conference announcement poster
Stefan Sagmeister

Stefan Sagmeister jokes, "I think the last class I took was yoga. My last design-related class was when my former intern gave me Photoshop lessons."

Sagmeister admits that he usually goes to conferences if he is asked to speak at them and then takes the opportunity to visit other panels. But in general, he does not attend design conferences. "There are few conferences where I really have the feeling I have learned. It is more like a sense of education than a true education."

There are exceptions. Sagmeister notes that he has often attended the Technology, Entertainment, Design (TED) conference in Monterey, which is about design, but, he comments, "[It is] much more about science." The cross-disciplinary atmosphere of such a meeting of people has the effect of stimulating the imagination in methods and practices (not to mention images) far outside the purview of design. In January 2003,

Sagmeister went to St. Mortiz to a conference where graphic designers were in the complete minority. "It was mostly product designers and educators, and I find that much more interesting. When there are people who do different things than I do, I learn from them."

Designer: Stefan Sagmeister

³⁹ Support young designers

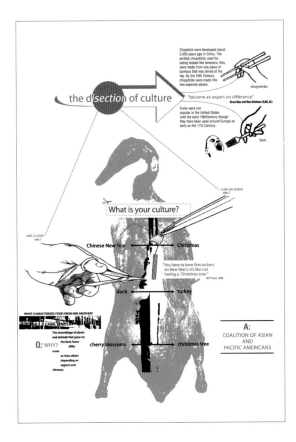

Student work
Worksight

Scott Santoro of Worksight was involved with the New York AIGA chapter, which kept him busy. "I served for two years as vice president, and I was really active. Since then, I started an AIGA student group at Pratt, which includes about 50 graduate and undergraduate students. We are able to attract good speakers, who also have a high-profile draw."

The students with whom Santoro works are interested in the wider industry of design, and this group gives them an opportunity to keep abreast of the variety of design-related events that happen all over New York City. Because the New York AIGA chapter is the largest in the country, and Pratt has the largest number of graphic design students of any school in the country, providing a group for students seemed like a natural outgrowth of Santoro's work with the New York City chapter and his interest in teaching.

The students attend talks by figures such as Jean Widmer and Stefan Sagmeister and discuss what they've seen and heard. Involvement in the group can be a good foundation for the résumé for a student just out of school—being involved with a professional organization demonstrates interest in the field as a whole. In addition, involvement in the group gives students an opportunity to make contacts with people in the industry while they are still in school. "It was easy for me to start because I had so many contacts already," says Santoro. "I think it is a good thing to provide students with this opportunity."

Designer: Loan Lam

When you retire, deal with the possibilities, not the necessities

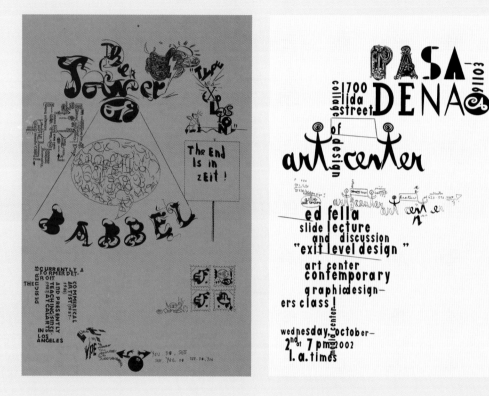

Announcement Flyers
Ed Fella

Ed Fella describes himself as an "exit-level" designer. He now co-teaches a general graduate-level graphic design seminar with first- and second-year students at California Institute of Arts (Cal Arts) in Valencia, California.

"The reason I do this is I'm retired. I'm not in the business anymore. I haven't done professional work for about 15 years, and I don't use a computer. I just make my own handmade pieces." Fella is also profoundly disinterested in business knowledge. He doesn't see the world of business today as any different than it was in the '50s, '60s, and '70s, when he was actively working. In addition, he doesn't know how to use a computer to do design—an essential element in the nuts-and-bolts education for design undergraduates today. "I don't really want to think about that anymore. It's part of the student's obligation to have to deal with professional practice, obviously. I have plenty of wisdom to impart, but I don't have so much knowledge anymore about the professional business and all the digital stuff. I enjoy my graduate seminar because there are other faculty involved with it. I can be kind of a grand old man of technical problems. Now I'm 65. I did teach full-time for about 13 years after my career in professional work."

Staying engaged with the creativity of his older students and colleagues and maintaining his own studio on the Cal Arts campus keep Fella involved with a somewhat rarified corner of the design world, but that is OK with him. "In the grad program at Cal Arts, we deal in the possibilities, not the necessities. In undergraduate education you have to teach people how to *be* graphic designers. Graduate education is more experimental. By the time you come to graduate education you already *are* a graphic designer. In graduate education you deal with possibilities and experimental stuff."

Designer, Illustrator: Ed Fella

㊶ Go back to school no matter how old you are

Announcement Flyers
Ed Fella

Ed Fella worked in Detroit at a large design studio for the first half of his career. He had received what he calls a "Bauhaus" model of high school education—a rigorous trade education larded liberally with humanities topics—and when he got out of high school he went right to work. "In Detroit in those days you did work in large studios. It wasn't like now when designers are in small shops or individuals. We had studios with 60 people in them—that was how the profession was in those days. I did that work for a long time. I did it honestly and wasn't cynical about it. My father was an autoworker. I didn't have any problem helping to sell the cars."

"I finally went back to graduate school. I was 48 and said, 'Well, now I can become a full-time teacher and end the professional design career.' It was that Detroit idea of 30 and up, that Walter Ruther thought up—that you would work for 30 years and then you'd retire. You wouldn't be burnt out, and another person would take your place. I also could retire from

professional design to teach, and I'd have time to do my personal work, which I've done since then. I'm famous now for my personal work, which is ironic—no one gives a shit about the 30 years of design work—the automotive industry, the heath care industry. These things are collectors' items now."

Designer, Illustrator: Ed Fella

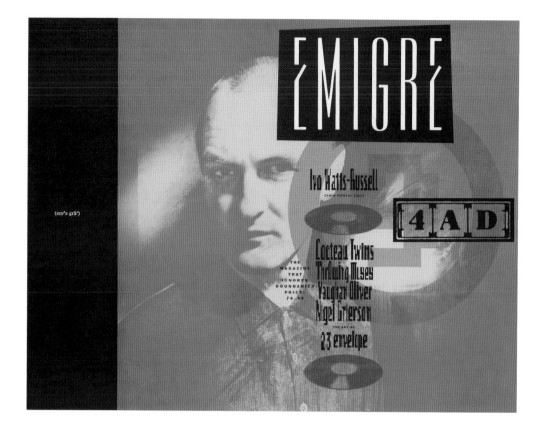

⓸ Start a magazine

Emigre magazine cover: issue 4
Rudy VanderLans and Zuzana Licko, Emigre

Rudy VanderLans and Zuzana Licko created *Emigre* magazine because they were unhappy with their regular jobs. VanderLans describes the foundation of Emigre as "a tediously slow process that would make for some very boring reading when retold in detail. Let's just say we were very naive, and we worked very long days." In addition to working on the magazine, which in its first years was published sporadically, Licko edited fonts for Adobe and VanderLans did design work for other magazines. Their company was called Emigre Graphics, and their magazine was a forge for their emerging styles.

VanderLans and Licko were quick to adopt the Macintosh computer as a design tool when it was first introduced, a move that ultimately propelled the magazine to a higher level. By being at the right place at the right time and applying her knowledge of font design to the new technology, Licko used the early bitmap design tools on the Macintosh to create some of the first digital fonts. Emperor, Oakland, and Emigre were designed for low-resolution printing and, by the third issue, became available for purchase. The sale of fonts has created enough economic flexibility that the magazine is now published quarterly.

It takes a sustained effort as well as a persistent and keen business acumen to run a magazine. In terms of creative return, however, for VanderLans, the magazine format offers everything a designer could wish for: a chance to mix texts of all kinds, images, and headlines and deal with sequencing of pages. "And every time you're done with one issue, you start afresh with the next one."

Designer: Rudy VanderLans

㊸ Make a low-budget project look expensive

Matteo Fine Linen identity and packaging
Chase Design Group

When Matteo's president, Matt Lenoci, first approached the Chase Design Group, Matteo had a logo and packaging scheme, but it was clearly in need of an update. The new logo is based on a classical roman serif font updated for a more modern feeling. Chase Design Group's solution for the packaging resolved two problems. The first problem was how to give the company a luxurious look without breaking its modest budget. The second was how to package the variety of sizes of product without requiring different-sized labels for each item. Chase Design Group created a single card-label printed on heavy rag stock, which is foil-stamped and embossed. These techniques would normally be prohibitively expensive, but Chase Design Group figured out a way to attach the same label to a variety of vinyl bag sizes using a grommet to hold the label to the center of the bag. This approach created a unique, high-end look for the products.

Chase Design Group also developed a series of postcard-sized info cards for each product that fit into a small custom binder of oversized fabric swatches, which allows the recipients to appreciate the full beauty of the fabrics. Expanding the concept of modern luxury across all of the company's materials established a cohesive brand that held up next to the competition and increased the integrity and appeal of the line for the consumer. As a result, selling Matteo to the end user became easier for the retailer.

Creative Director: Margo Chase
Designers: Margo Chase, Patricia Guerra
Illustrator: Margo Chase
Photography: Victor Bracke
Studio: Chase Design Group
Client: Matteo Fine Linen

㊹ Read it all, forget it all, and do your own thing

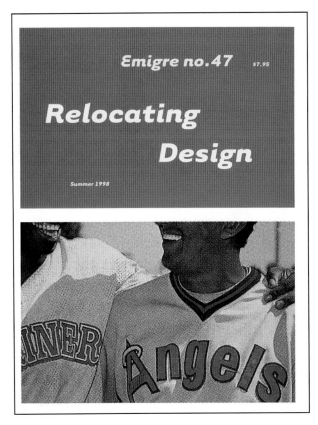

Emigre magazine covers: issue 48, issue 37, issue 47, issue 46
Rudy VanderLans and Zuzana Licko, Emigre

Because of their unique position as designers who make a magazine, advice from Rudy VanderLans and Zuzana Licko can be hard to categorize. "If you want to know how to set up a graphic design studio, you should probably talk to people like Milton Glaser or Pentagram," Vanderlans demurs. Citing their longevity, he supposes they must be doing something right.

Although Emigre does not follow the conventional model of a client-based studio, the insights VanderLans and Licko are able to offer are nonetheless useful, particularly for people who are just getting started. In some sense, Emigre's work is the purest entrepreneurial model you can find—they create their own products and do their own sales and distribution. This style of business flies in the face of a conventional shop that depends on client work for its revenue and the direction of its work. Emigre essentially eschews dependence upon the client and the web of commercial acceptance. By developing a catalog of fonts and concentrating on the magazine, VanderLans and Licko keep themselves busy with the kind of work that challenges and satisfies them. They located a niche within the magazine market and filled it with what they wanted to see.

Designer: Rudy VanderLans

㊺ Actively pursue intellectual subjects that resonate with you

Psychedelic Language poster
Worksight

"I'm constantly getting involved with subjects that interest me, working months at a time, reading everything I can about it," says Scott Santoro of Worksight. This kind of intellectual curiosity drives him to research everything from psychedelia to Wittgenstein.

For a lecture about the art of the psychedelic poster, Santoro worked with a friend from Dartmouth College. "He wanted me to give a talk for a show about psychedelic poster art for which he was designing the graphics. I read everything I could find about the subject. I called every designer I knew who might know something about it. I talked to Kathy McCoy, who, it turned out, designed psychedelic posters when she was a college student, and included her posters in the lecture. I spoke with people who were graphic designers during that time period. I also located a psychedelic typography catalog that was floating around New York, so I included that in the lecture. My friend asked me to do it from a graphic designer's point of view. The result was that a textile client of mine asked me if I had any

lectures I would like to present for the Color Council in New York. It is so great to have someone ask you to give a talk like this because it forces you to learn and establish your own opinions and theories about a subject."

Santoro views this interest as ongoing; he has put the latest draft of his essay on the company Web site (www.worksight.com) to generate discussion and to spread the materials more widely.

Designer: Scott Santoro/Worksight

㊻ Learn the vernacular of a new field

Brooklyn Business Library brochure
Worksight

"I had just finished a piece for Gilbert paper which was about the subculture of sturgeon spearing, and I brought it along to my meeting at the Brooklyn Business Library. The director there really liked it, and I knew I had the project just by her exuberance about it," Scott Santoro recalls when discussing an award-winning brochure he created for this small, specialized library.

The sturgeon-spearing piece was based on the subculture of people around Lake Winnebago who create small houses to drag out on to the ice each winter. Santoro hired a guide to bring him around the lake and spent some time watching the preparations, as well as the fishing itself. By learning about the traditions of this chilly pastime, he was able to accurately reflect the obsessions of the activity and speak its visual vernacular in the final piece.

In the environment of the library, where the subculture revolves around access to and mastery of information, Scott went in with a similar, sociologically focused view. "I knew the people who

ran the library were a very proud bunch. I spent three days with a copywriter and photographer doing interviews and finding vignettes of people who use the library." Libraries are often, ironically, lackluster about graphic design, especially considering the fact that books and the communication of information is the central task of such institutions. The brochure he created ended up winning numerous awards within the library system, so its effectiveness as a tool to speak to experts in the field was clear. In addition, it is a beautiful and intricate piece that works very hard despite its diminutive size. It also achieves the goal of introducing and orienting newcomers to the library in a hands-on manner. "I think it shows how much I like the library too," says Scott. By incorporating language that was specific to the library and to library patrons, Scott learned more about how business organizes information and how to better access that information in a visual manner.

Designer: Scott Santoro/Worksight

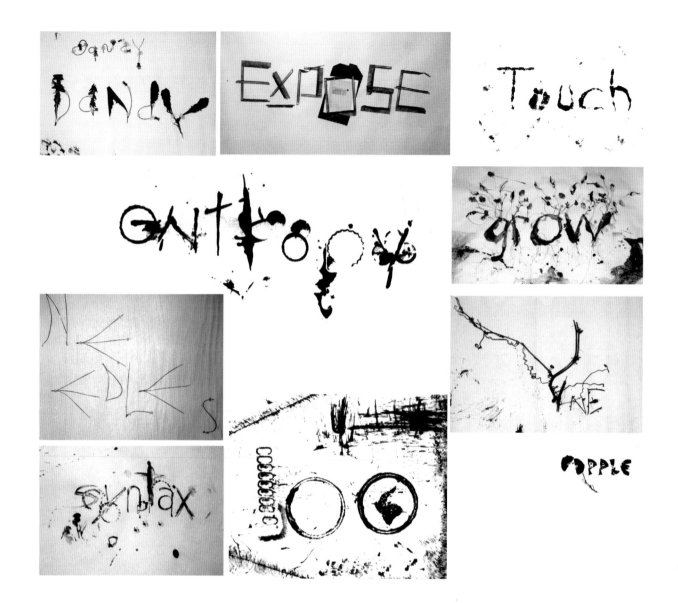

㊼ Continue your own education by teaching

Dirty Words workshop
Chase Design Group

In addition to teaching Type 4 at Cal Arts, Los Angeles, designer Margo Chase also gives workshops from time to time. "I find it very satisfying," she notes. "It gives me a different perspective on the practice of design."

Dirty Words was a project that Chase did at a design conference in Nebraska called "Art Farm." About 40 local designers participated in workshops presented by several prominent visiting designers. The point was to escape the routine of the standard workday and get inspired.

Chase provided large pieces of white paper and pots of India ink. She asked the participants to search the grounds around the hotel and collect objects. They then had to use these objects to create letters and words. They could write by dipping the objects in ink, using them as stamps, or simply gluing them down. The participants raided trash cans, pulled weeds, and made ink stains on the carpet, all in the name of creative expression.

Art Director: Margo Chase
Designers: Various workshop participants
Studio: Chase Design Group
Client: Nebraska AIGA

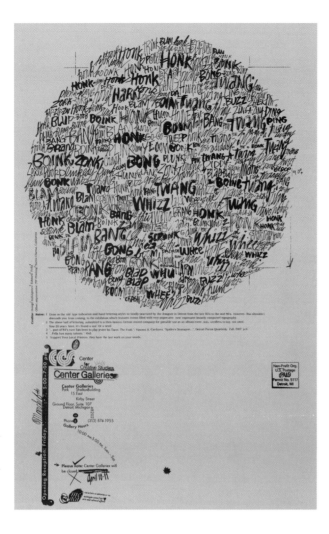

⁴⁸ Develop and sustain an art practice throughout your life

Announcement Flyers
Ed Fella

Ed Fella occupies a unique position as a retired designer, functioning somewhere on the edges of the design world but not fully in it. "I've carved out this odd position where I'm still a graphic designer using graphic design but as an art practice. Graphic design has to have a subject, a deadline—all of that. With these pieces, I'm the subject—it's the opposite of graphic design, where the artist is never the subject. The designer is never the subject."

Fella recently published *Letters from America*, a collection of his Polaroid photographs of lettering and surfaces. In addition to this, he has a backlog of work that he hopes to eventually get out into the public world. "I have a bunch of books sitting here, but I haven't really gotten around to them. I have one all on faces and landscapes. They are signs or windows, or posters with faces and landscapes painted on them. Polaroid format. I have thousands of those. My wife has put them together and edited them, but we haven't gone to any publishers. I have about 80 sketchbooks with 100 drawings in each one. They are

shown here and there, but they haven't been published. I like to make stuff, I don't really like to put it together. It is always such a pain in the ass, just to send stuff to shows. I get plenty of calls, so I haven't gone out there and pushed." Although he supported himself doing conventional graphic design for many years, Ed Fella's personal work has been his most enjoyable, as well as his most successful and critically regarded.

Designer, Illustrator: Ed Fella

㊾ Never stop learning; don't start teaching

adidas "Forever Sport" print advertising
Miles Murray Sorrell FUEL

The Miles Murray Sorrell FUEL team has never been drawn to teaching at art schools. Instead, they feel that they provide a good insight into their graphic sensibility as designers through their books. They continue to learn by producing work in ways that push the boundaries of their knowledge and keep their interest keen.

"We set up and photographed the adidas ad one morning in a local community sports hall. This ad was part of a European adidas campaign in which artists and designers were asked to come up with an image based around the line 'Forever Sport.' This campaign gave us the opportunity to generate an image for adidas that was not focused on a specific product or personality. We used the sculpture of our studio contents from our book (*FUEL 3000*, pp. 20 and 21) as a starting point. In the local community sports hall, we constructed a similar sculpture using the sporting equipment we found on the premises and added various adidas products."

By relating a commercial project to a more personal, noncommercial project, FUEL moves what might otherwise be a conventional shoe advertisement into a new realm, appropriating the products as elements in their own art, rather than allowing the product to dictate the content.

Designers: Miles Murray Sorrell FUEL

㊿ Encourage young people to make art

Yoda illustrations
John C Jay, Wieden+Kennedy, Tokyo

John C Jay rarely participates in design conferences in Japan; rather, he concentrates his professional development on speaking with small groups or doing internal presentations for clients. In addition, he works with *Illustration* magazine to develop and encourage young talent.

"I just personally judged 2,000 pieces of art that were sent to *Illustration* magazine. I'm very involved with them in encouraging young artists. Most recently, they did a call for entries for young artists in Japan. I wrote a brief, and the first thing they said to me was, 'Your client is Nike—why don't you do something like designing a new sneaker, a new Nike shoe?' I'm not here to train them for a career; I'm here to motivate them to think about the world in a way that perhaps they haven't before. One of the outlets is self-expression—to answer the question, why be an artist? And so I said in my brief, 'God—which ever one you believe in—has given us the ability to have emotions and to express those emotions. You have been blessed with another ability, which is a physical ability of some kind of artistic

skill with which to express ideas. Express to me the most powerful emotion that you are feeling at the moment. Don't make it about trendiness and style. Don't worry if it is a cool technique. Don't worry about whether it is something that your teacher or employer said you couldn't do. Don't worry if it is a thing that doesn't sell. Just forget all that, and express the most powerful emotion in your body right now.'"

For the special competition, "expressing your emotions," the magazine received more than 500 entries. Jay spent hours looking through and judging them; he then made a presentation of the 15 that he chose, and they were featured in the magazine. Hiroyuki Yoda, whose work is featured here, was chosen by Jay as the first place winner. This contribution to the creative lives of the young artists of Japan is essential to the work Jay performs as a creative director. Through this project, he networks with a publication and lends his talents to their creative direction. He also stays in touch with Japan's nascent emerging talent.

Illustrations: Hiroyuki Yoda

5

51-63
Community Involvement

The way a designer defines "community" and "community involvement" varies greatly because of the range of experience each person brings to the field. For some, "community" means the design community—professional organizations, colleagues, students—but for others, it means participation in the wider civic circle of their city, their country, or the world. The role that designers create for themselves as community members determines what they feel they can or should give back to the community. Despite the differences in time or economic resources, designers can always find a way to have a positive effect on their community. This chapter illustrates some case studies of designers and firms who have developed an effective balance in their art to both create commercial work and work that "gives back."

(51) Develop a social agenda

Sphere magazine
Mark Randall, Worldstudio, Inc., and Worldstudio Foundation

The unique integration of Worldstudio, Inc. and the Worldstudio Foundation sets this organization apart. David Sterling and Mark Randall started the foundation before creating their design studio. Their goal was to have a business, but they first wanted to prioritize the mission of the nonprofit organization that became the Worldstudio Foundation. They discovered that it was impossible to merge the interests of a business with their socially active work, so the foundation and Worldstudio, Inc. developed as distinct entities.

The umbrella mission of the foundation is to involve creative professionals in socially and environmentally aware projects. The most overt manifestation of the foundation work is the magazine *Sphere*, which is published approximately once a year and features projects of the foundation as well as global concerns of the foundation. The magazine is a forum for the creative work of Worldstudio and provides ongoing inspiration for the staff of the design studio. It is also the arena in which the cross-pollination between the studio and the foundation occurs.

Specific foundation initiatives include a scholarship program with an emphasis on supporting diversity and support for creative people who build a social agenda into their work in some way. The foundation also has a mentorship program in which creative professionals are paired to work on community-based projects. For example, high school students team up with working graphic designers and artists to create billboards against gun violence, a newspaper on homophobia, or a poster series on tolerance. The end results are displayed in the public arena. Through these programs, high school students are exposed to a variety of career opportunities and are able to learn how they can use the power of creativity to give back to their communities.

Everything that the foundation does nurtures the idea of making artists and designers—whether they be high-school-aged students, college students, or professionals—more socially and environmentally aware and giving them tools, ideas, and inspiration to use their creativity for positive social change.

WISH YOU WERE HERE

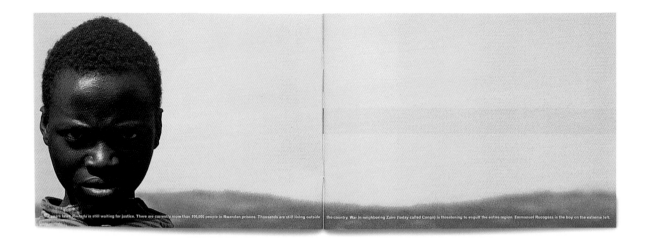

Two years later, Rwanda is still waiting for justice. There are currently more than 100,000 people in Rwandan prisons. Thousands are still living outside the country. War in neighboring Zaire (today called Congo) is threatening to engulf the entire region. Emmanuel Rucogoza is the boy on the extreme left.

2001 Sphere magazine—Wish You Were Here
Editorial Directors: Mark Randall, David Sterling
Art Directors: Mark Randall, David Sterling
Editors: Peter Hall, Emmy Kondo
Designers: Sven Oberstein
Illustrators: Various
Photography: Various
Client: Worldstudio Foundation

2000 Sphere magazine—Boundaries
Editorial Directors: Mark Randall, David Sterling
Art Directors: Mark Randall, David Sterling
Editors: Peter Hall, Emmy Kondo
Designers: Mark Randall, Noreen Leahey
Illustrators: Various
Photography: Various
Client: Worldstudio Foundation

1997 Sphere magazine
Editorial Directors: Mark Randall, David Sterling
Art Directors: Mark Randall, David Sterling
Editor: Peter Hall
Designers: Stefan Hengst, Tom Kohen, Chika Azuma, Naomi Mizusaki
Illustrators: Various
Photography: Various
Client: Worldstudio Foundation

⑤² Develop long-term relationships with nonprofit organizations

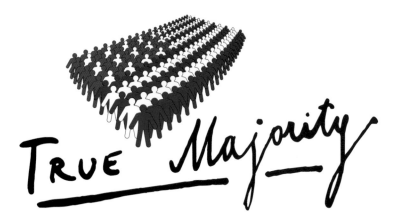

True Majority promotional materials
Stefan Sagmeister

Sagmeister aims to do about a third of its work for socially relevant causes. In 2002, Sagmeister teamed up with True Majority—a group of 500 business people under the leadership of Ben Cohen, one of the founders of Ben and Jerry's Ice Cream—who had put together a 10-point program to influence national leadership in left-leaning political causes. Some members see it as a preventative measure against another 9/11; some see it as a plan for the United States to improve its behavior in the world; some see it as a group that makes the world a better place. It is a program with very wide goals–some specific, like paying U.N. dues willingly; some vast, like trying to solve the problem of world hunger.

Although True Majority didn't get off the ground until late 2002, Sagmeister started working on this project in 2001, doing everything from identity packages and brochures to cars that travel the East Coast drawing attention to the cause.

At first, Sagmeister worked for True Majority for free, but the workload became so massive that they either had to recommend True Majority to somebody else or get paid for the overhead costs of doing the project. Fortunately, the client was able to afford the reduced rate. Sagmeister stuck with the project because it not only reflects his political values but also allows him significant creative freedom.

Designer: Stefan Sagmeister

⑤³ Address local, immediate needs

Fight Back NY! post-9/11 economic support campaign
Mark Randall, Worldstudio, Inc.

Although the Worldstudio Foundation is wholly devoted to the aims of education and empowerment, Worldstudio, Inc. limits its involvement with social causes.

Worldstudio feels a commitment to support community need. Located in New York, Worldstudio was in the thick of the fallout from 9/11. When one of their clients, a business improvement district in New York, asked them to contribute some time on a pro-business, pro-downtown project, they felt compelled to respond and help in the most effective manner they could. Worldstudio created messaging that conveyed a return to life as normal—and not just any life, but a fun-loving life with shopping and going to the theater—in a visual landscape that was devastated and a business climate of severe dislocation and decline. Worldstudio created buttons, banners, posters, and T-shirts, which were very popular and copied widely all over the city. Like Milton Glaser's "I [heart] New York More Than Ever," this campaign shows a team of designers responding to

a very local, very fundamental need within their own community. It not only went a long way in providing a visual reminder of hope, but its relevance also gave the designers a sense of satisfaction in being able to help so close to home.

Art Director, Designer: Mark Randall
Client: The Fashion Center

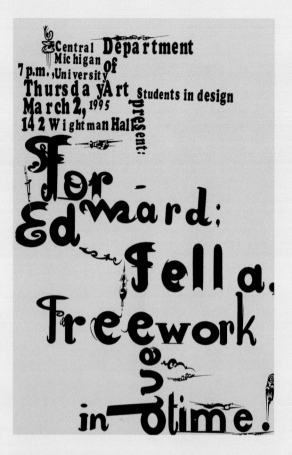

⑤④ Use the Robin Hood theory

Announcement Flyer
Ed Fella

Ed Fella worked throughout the '70s for arts organizations in and around Detroit. In addition to designing *Detroit Focus Quarterly*, a local art magazine, he did thousands of posters on which he would execute his typographic experiments. He contributed his design time as well as the facilities of the shop in which he was working. To get new typefaces, which at that time had to be purchased, he would piggyback the typeface from a paying job onto pro bono jobs. "I'd do a job for a car company for which we'd put on a few lines of type and send it out, so I'd get the type. I'd use the studio facilities. I couldn't have done that work if I didn't have a job. I couldn't be a starving artist and do this pro bono work. I never made a penny on it. Now it costs so little, I never have to pay much for printing. You know, I make 100 copies and it only costs 50 bucks. If it were a real project, it would cost thousands of dollars to print."

"My work for nonprofits was entirely based on the fact that I had this big studio at my fingertips. I had the board to do the mechanicals, type, wax, pencils—all of that. I would always give credit to the company I worked at—they didn't mind. It wasn't like I was taking work money away from them. They probably threw more stuff away than I used for the arts organization anyway. I robbed Peter to pay Paul."

Designer, Illustrator: Ed Fella

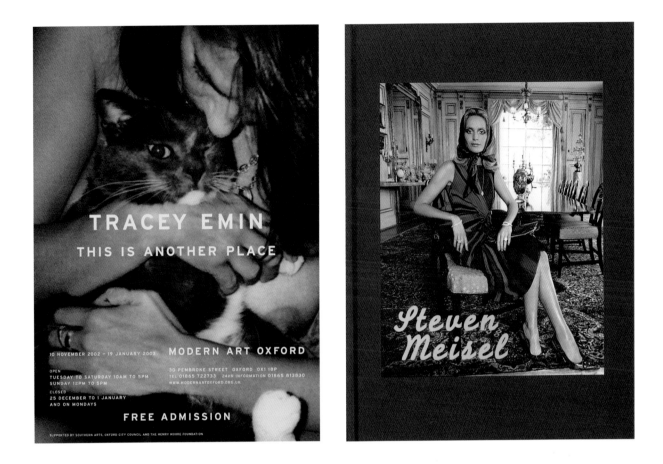

⑤ Minimize travel expenses—work with your neighbors

Tracey Emin poster, Steven Meisel book cover
Miles Murray Sorrell FUEL

Miles Murray Sorrell FUEL has worked for the White Cube art gallery in nearby Hoxton Square in London for the last two years. "The Steven Meisel catalog is just one of the catalogs we have designed for their shows. We started working with Tracey Emin, who lives a few doors down from our studio, through our work with White Cube. We designed the poster and invitation for her New York show and all related material for her Oxford show including poster, leaflets, and catalog. We continue to work with her on major publications of her work," notes Damon Murray.

Designers: Miles Murray Sorrell FUEL
Photography: Tracey Emin (left), Steven Meisel (right)

⑤⑥ Create highly visible and culturally consequential design by working for clients in education and the arts

Kumon campaign
John C Jay, Wieden+Kennedy, Tokyo

One of Wieden+Kennedy's clients in Tokyo is the Kumon Learning Institute, which teaches a particular method of learning mathematics and languages. John C Jay notes, "One of the reasons we opened in Japan is to really tie into areas that were socially and culturally significant. One of the great areas of change is the educational system."

As of April 2002, Japanese children no longer had six school days a week. Japanese families suddenly had free time on Saturdays, forever transforming the way that people think about education. Jay notes, "Now that parents have to take responsibility for their children, they're asking, 'What do I do with that extra day?' 'Do I give it to them for free time?' 'Do give them other types of education, in sports or arts?' 'Do I send them to a cram school or a Kumon Institute?' 'What do I do with that day that formerly was used for education?'"

In addition to this massive change in the school week, the Japanese were also experiencing a movement that advocated children's self-sufficiency and free thinking. "Kumon is a great outlet for us to talk about these issues," Jay notes. Any involvement in the change in educational structures is fundamental to the change in Japanese culture.

Wieden+Kennedy also undertook a recent project with Mori Building, a preeminent builder in Japan, which has helped secure their place of status in the art world. Mori Building is launching the largest-ever post-war redevelopment of a 28-acre area in Tokyo called Roppongi Hills. The centerpiece of this development is a 53-story tower, with the top five floors devoted to the arts. In developing the branding and strategic thinking for Roppongi Hills, Jay knew that the museum and galleries would be an important symbolic and cultural beacon. "Our first assignment was working with Mori Building as strategic planners, as design consultants. One of the first tangible things we did was a mission statement book for everyone who works at Roppongi Hills to help them understand how this city will be different—how and why it is not just a real estate development, what the mission statement of Mr. Mori is, what the goals of building this city are. The city was already under construction when we got on board. It took 15 years to make this city, to buy up all the leases, and to negotiate all the land contracts, which is a very tedious and complicated process in Tokyo. Being involved in the mission statement for the city itself has been a wonderful exercise intellectually, sitting there with the president and talking about the motivations behind this project, how it is going to be different, how it is going to tap into the rest of Tokyo and the rest of the world."

Creative Director: John C Jay, Sumiko Sato
Art Director: Hiroshi Yonemura
Designer: Akihiro Tanabe (Watch)
Photography: Kazunari Tajima
Copywriter: Megumi Ohta

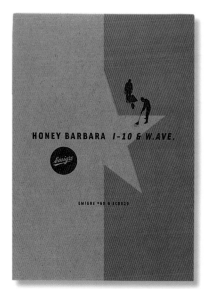

㊹ Integrate your politics with your creation

Emigre magazine: issue 60
Rudy VanderLans and Zuzana Licko, Emigre

Rudy VanderLans of Emigre has discovered that doing projects for nonprofit organizations is not the only way to give back to the community. He believes that anyone can be of great service to society by simply considering the impact that daily actions have on society and the environment and acting accordingly. For example, a graphic designer can align himself or herself with clients—and not necessarily nonprofit clients—that contribute in a positive way. VanderLans notes, "If it wasn't for so many exploitative, wasteful, and obscenely unscrupulous businesses, there would hardly be a need for nonprofits because they usually exist to right the many wrongs created by the aforementioned businesses."

Emigre is unique because its designers do not run a service-oriented business—they create their own products. Thus, their responsibilities involve how they use their resources. "I am proud that our catalogs and magazines are often printed on paper with very high recycled content and are often processed

chlorine-free, which is much more expensive than nonrecycled paper. This represents a more direct way to support environmental causes than giving money to, let's say, Earth First, or doing pro bono work for them," says VanderLans.

In addition, the magazine provides a unique forum for communicating with the public. Emigre feels a degree of responsibility toward their design community, and they take their work seriously. In the magazine, they write about design, about the process, and about its effect on culture. "I think it is healthy for graphic design to have this constant probe going on. To look at what motivates designers, to question the work—we can all learn from each other. We're proud of contributing to that in a small way."

Designer: Rudy VanderLans

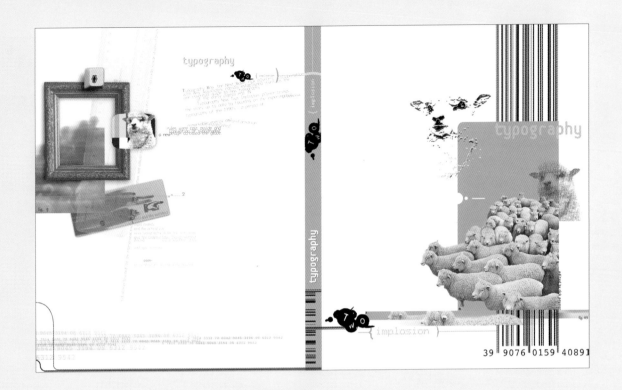

⑤⑧ Teach

Student work
Worksight

In economic terms, being an adjunct instructor is a bum deal. The days are long, and the work can be taxing. In emotional terms, it is a labor of love that returns to its practitioner a sense of satisfaction and accomplishment rarely found in other pursuits.

Although Scott Santoro and his partner, Emily, have been teaching one class each term at Pratt for the past six years, they do not do it for the money. "In terms of the output of our little company, it is a lot," Santoro notes. But the payback is enormous.

"One of my students was discussing deconstruction with another professor, and the professor said, 'You should go talk to Scott about that.' So I invited the student over for an hour. We talked, and I showed him work. I think he went away even more confused than when he got here. It is OK though; critical conversations tend to be like that. The great thing for me was that we were both intellectually engaged in the middle of a workday. How many people can claim that during the week?

I see students really take off with their work. Helping to set the wheels in motion for them is wonderful because they come back to you years later with their eyes glowing, so happy to see you, thanking you for helping them with a piece of something—more than just the job of design. That's what makes it worth it."

Designer: Loan Lam

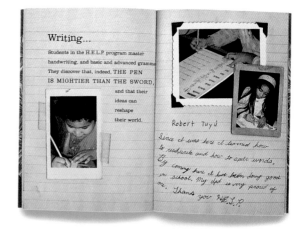

Don't feel obligated to do charity work

Hollywood Education and Literacy Project (HELP)
Chase Design Group

"I don't believe anyone is obligated to do charity or pro bono work," remarks Margo Chase. "It is a choice that we have the luxury to make because the business is successful enough to be able to give away work and still provide for our staff. If I had to choose between my ability to provide for the people who work here and doing pro bono work, I would choose the staff."

Although she does not believe that designers have any greater responsibility to society and the culture at large than other professionals, the Chase Design Group does work with the Hollywood Education and Literacy Project (HELP) annual fund-raising campaign.

"I strongly believe in supporting literacy education. HELP provides reading instruction to anyone who needs it—old, young, rich, or poor. Everyone's enthusiastic and excited, and they have a terrific success rate. They allow us to bring our own vision to their promotions, so we have a lot of creative freedom. In addition, several friends and a few clients support them, so it's an easy relationship for us."

Two pieces that the firm created recently are part of a continuing series of books about HELP. Chase Design Group mailed these pieces to a list of friends and supporters of HELP in the hopes

of raising money, and they have been very successful so far. Each book focuses on a different aspect of HELP. The first piece provides an overview of the program using existing shots of kids and their written testimonials. Chase wanted it to have a hand-made, intimate feel—a little like a reading primer or storybook. The second one focuses on a compelling case study involving a child with ADD. Both pieces present HELP's work in a friendly but realistic way, without shouting or banner waving. Chase Design Group felt it was important to capture the personal, one-on-one nature of their teaching and coaching by presenting each piece in an intimate style.

Despite her work with HELP, Chase notes, "I think doing free work is a burden for many small firms who are just scraping by. We are a much larger business now and profitable enough to be able to put resources to work for free when we choose."

Left
Creative Director and Designer: Margo Chase
Photography: Michael Doven

Right
Creative Director: Margo Chase
Designer, Illustrator: Maria Gaviria

"D̃ERANGED"?

I felt I had no way out, and agreed to have him be part of a research study for ADD medication.

"WANDERING CHILD?"

"ATTENTION DEFICIT DISORDER?"

They called him a *wandering child* always day-dreaming. He may suffer from some sort of "Attention Deficit Disorder" the teachers suggested. If you look up the word disorder it means a *disruption; a breach of public peace; a riot; a disregard of system; ill; deranged.* My beautiful child "deranged?"

I did my best to tutor him, but soon Fabian was given evaluations at school. The teachers felt he may fail again.

"Hollywood Education and Literacy Project."

I began to read. As I read about the project, I began to see a brighter future for my son. I made an appointment for the next day.

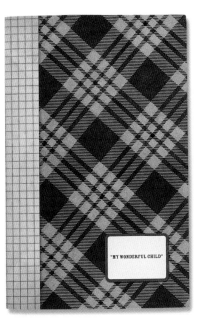

"MY WONDERFUL CHILD"

Keep in touch with your nonprofit clients

Amanaka'a newsletter
Worksight

Scott Santoro of Worksight had worked with an organization called Amanaka'a, which supported tribal people in the Amazon region. Santoro helped them create a newsletter every three or four months and designed T-shirts.

The organization ended up folding, in part because they were competing against a much bigger organization—the Rainforest Network—which was started by the musician Sting and had a much more mainstream cachet and popularity. Fortunately for Santoro, many of the people from Amanaka'a followed their political convictions to the Rainforest Network. Santoro got a call from the Rainforest Network about a possible job. It turned out that they needed an annual report and a calendar, and, because of the ties he had forged years before, he was able to show his work at the new organization. They ended up awarding him the project. "They don't pay like a corporation would pay, but they do have a budget. Of course, they will be getting a good deal, because they will be getting a ton of energy from me," Santoro says.

Designer: Scott Santoro/Worksight

61 Partner with like-minded firms

Worldstudio capabilities brochure
Worksight

"An average amount of money was involved in this project but an above-average amount of my own interest, because my work was for a cause I really believe in. I enjoy working with an organization that has values so near to my own thinking about design and design education," comments Scott Santoro on his collaboration with Worldstudio, Inc.

Worksight and Worldstudio, Inc. collaborated on a project because Scott Santoro knew David Sterling from his old studio, Doublespace. "Cranbrook grads knew about that studio because he and Jane Kostrin were past graduates of the school and were able to create a successful practice in New York City," Santoro says.

While Santoro was on the board of the New York AIGA chapter, he met with Sterling to see how AIGA and Worldstudio might support each other in fostering design education. When Sterling was planning a fund-raising auction for Worldstudio, Inc., he asked Worksight to contribute a piece, which they did, and it was auctioned for a few hundred dollars. When Sterling and Mark Randall were thinking of bringing another designer in to help reinvent their newsletter and capabilities brochure, they thought of Worksight.

Santoro says, "I was really honored that they asked. I respect and keep all the Worldstudio promotions sent to me over the years and consider their approach to be similar to my own. They aren't afraid of form and enjoy presenting rich text and graphics. We were immediately on the same page. They also hired a good writer, Rachel Kash, as part of the brochure project, which meant that we could build something that both said and read in conceptual harmony."

Developing political alliances can work to the advantage of a designer, particularly when allied organizations share aesthetic styles.

Designer: Scott Santoro/Worksight

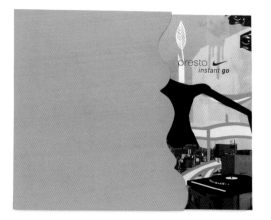

⑥² Use client work to collaborate with young new artists

Presto 4
John C Jay, Wieden+Kennedy, Tokyo

Campaigns for Nike Japan garnered respect and admiration for Wieden+Kennedy, Tokyo, even though they are a relatively young and Western-owned business. Creative director John C Jay cites his company's involvement with the most exciting young artists in Asia and the United States as some of his primary inspirations. "The idea for Presto for the last two seasons has been the idea behind the shoe itself, the idea of 'instant go,' which encourages young people—and all people—to be physically active, mentally active, socially active, and creatively active."

Jay asked Storm, a.k.a. David Ellis from the Barnstormers in New York, to be the artistic director for the Presto work. "He represents the whole post-graffiti generation of artists who are internationally famous on the street, known around the world to young people," explains Jay. With his help, Wieden+Kennedy chose a young painter, Sasuke, from the Naka Meguro area of Tokyo, as well as a Chinese painter named Frek. They next asked an up-and-coming Japanese DJ to participate. "We assembled everyone in a giant studio in Los Angeles, built glass walls, and had each painter respond to the others. They painted on top of moving images from Shanghai and Tokyo, responded to the music of DJ Uppercut, and responded to each other, and each one spurred the other one on. It was a three day, non-stop, collaboration of painting and creation."

In addition to the artists, Jay added team members who were experts in motion graphics and digital technology. "We used our knowledge of technology, very much inspired by Presto, very much inspired by Nike's way of working, with their famous R&D labs, always adding technology to our artistic endeavors, and what we helped these painters to do is lift their art off the two-dimensional wall and make it travel in three dimensions throughout the cities in Japan and China. We created a DVD and a two-minute commercial that we aired in Japan." This collaboration not only provided Nike with a truly fresh look, but also helped to elevate up-and-coming artists.

Creative Directors: John C Jay, Sumiko Sato
Art Directors: Eric Cruz, David Ellis
Copywriter: Barton Corley
Agency Producer: Kenji Tanaka
Account Executive: Fukmiko Horiuchi
Artists: Skwerm, Sasu, Frek, Motion Theory

63 Provide service to your design community

AIGA New York poster
Worksight

Working with the New York chapter of AIGA allowed Scott Santoro of Worksight to do work that he found really exciting and interesting. He saw his involvement with AIGA as a chance to actually follow though with some of his ideas about lectures he wanted to give and speakers he wanted to see. He was first asked to be on the "Fresh Dialogue" speakers series in 1991, and this opportunity provided the impetus for his involvement. Santoro's board service came out of an interest to create events at which members could extend their understanding of design. "One of the first events that I chaired involved Ed Fella and Massimo Vignelli, not because they were two famous 'celebrity' designers, but because they were the two most obsessive-compulsive designers I could think of to pair for what I named 'obsessive-compulsive design,' OCD."

Although it took up a lot of his time, Santoro learned a lot about event management—how to get people to attend events and how to work with a board of directors. Santoro felt the experience was important to his development as a member of a wider design community in New York. "The administrator at the New York chapter was worried about my spending too much time working for the chapter, but I really wanted to put some good time in during my tenure. I knew I was getting something back that I couldn't put a price tag on."

Designers: Ed Fella (left), Scott Santoro/Worksight (right)

64-76
Technology

Technological innovation has made it possible for designers to work in ways that were once practically or financially out of reach. Computer technology has expanded the capacities of many designers, helping them to develop new skills and gain experience in fields such as motion graphics, digital font development, and video editing. It has also streamlined the way designers and clients communicate, and it has provided designers in different fields with a new mode of communication.

Although computer technology has clearly altered the aesthetics and basic function of graphic design since the 1980s, it is difficult to state where the computer fits on a list of tools used by a designer because it seems to dominate so ruthlessly. The designers we interviewed all acknowledged the change that the computer has wrought on the field, but they were of very different minds as to its ultimate use.

All had opinions about "technology," but not all of them considered the computer to be the exhaustive definition of this concept.

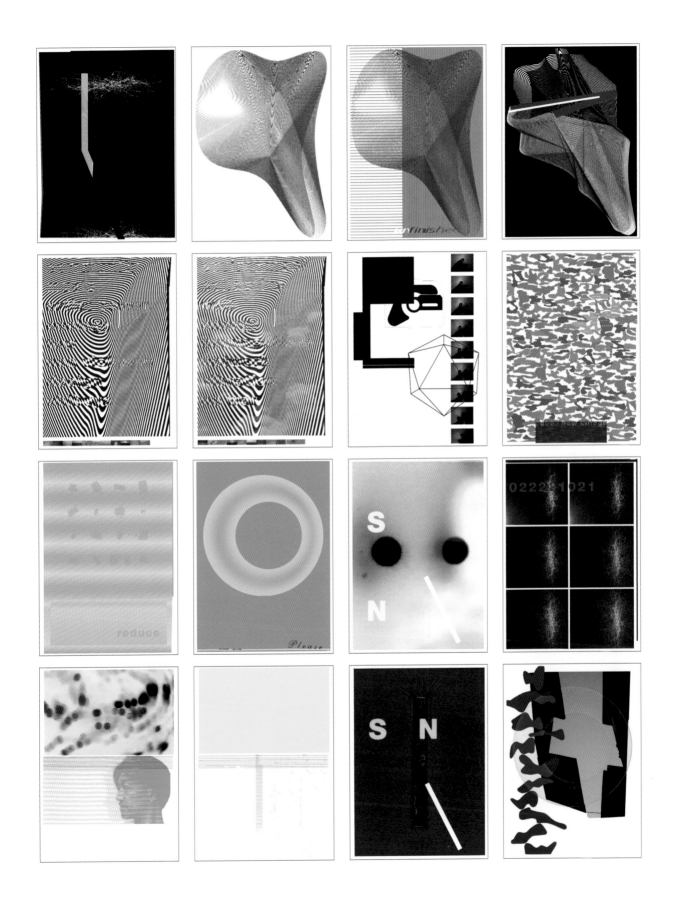

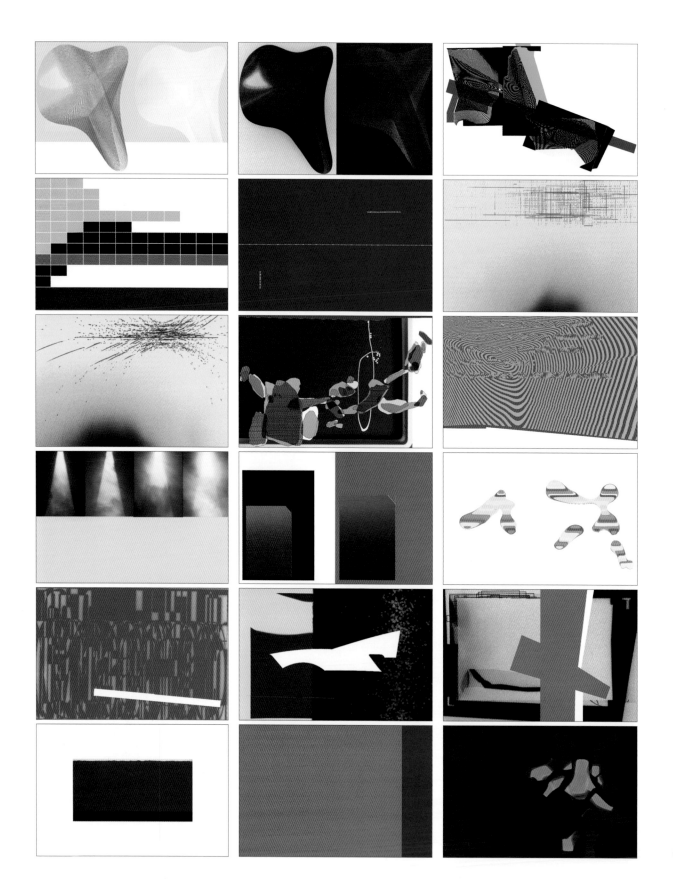

⑥④ Acknowledge the value of the analog process

"re-cycling"
Hideki Nakajima

Like any comparable design firm anywhere in the world, Hideki Nakajima's office in Tokyo has Macintosh G4s. Nakajima himself, however, does not use these machines. He comments, "I cannot use a Macintosh, but there is no problem because the staff can. Just as the invention of the electric guitar and synthesizer gave birth to rock-n-roll and techno music, and the invention of the projector gave birth to film, new technology bears new means of expression. I'm trying to seek out the possibilities of new technology." This seemingly contradictory stance, which lauds technology as a catalyst and yet shies away from its use, stands at the center of Nakajima's approach to the process of graphic design.

Nakajima is no Luddite. On the contrary, his work is highly engaged with the way information is processed visually. Rather than impeding creativity, Nakajima feels that technology is a direct result of creativity. He notes, "I think the final state of the development of technology is the human being. For example, robots are improved to become more and more like a human being. Digital processes are inferior to analog. They only enhance design; they cannot replace it. Creativity starts with the human mind and hand."

In his piece "re-cycling," which consists of 40 pieces created for the Japanese design magazine *IDEA* in 2002, Nakajima reconstructed all of his work from the past into refigured designs. Although he calls his work "meaningless," the complex conceptual framework for this series suggests that the reconfiguration and re-presentation of these highly abstracted images are as useful a process as their initial creation.

The reproduction of images by hand, through photographic or other processes, also influences Nakajima's images. He views computer-aided design as simply another way of treating an image, not more or less significant than other types of technological forms of reproduction. Each kind of reproductive process inserts its own meaning into the image, whether it is in a darkroom or at a copy machine. In fact, it is the fallibility of other technologies (particularly photography) that fascinates Nakajima, and he relishes accidents of color and light that can appear when using these methods.

Art Director, Designer: Hideki Nakajima
Photography: Akira Kitajima, Shigemi Tsutsumi, Mikiya Takimoto
Client: IDEA magazine

65 Use computers to communicate with stone masons

A Flock of Words
Why Not Associates

As part of a larger project for the small community of
Morecambe, Why Not created a 300-yard (274 m) sidewalk out
of type, steel, and stone. "A Flock of Words," as the path project
is called, was a collaborative project between Why Not
Associates, artist Gordon Young, and sculptor Russell Coleman.

"One of the reasons why this project was possible is technology," explains Andy Altmann of Why Not Associates. "I can give
a disk to a steel manufacturer, and he can use that disk to cut
out all the words using a laser. Also, a quarry can take the same
file and sand-blast granite for us. You'd never be able to do this
by hand—it would have taken forever, chiseling out all the lettering. Even five years ago, you couldn't have handed them a
disk to work from. Technology is working in strange ways, in
antiquated areas. For example, stone masonry is making a
comeback, and I find that quite fascinating. It is like learning to
print all over again. Stone has a permanence about it that is
interesting. To be able to walk over it and past it and around
it—it is more interesting than a book."

The pathway, which is over 8.25 feet (2.5 m) wide and just over
350 yards (320 m) long, serves as a connection between the
railway station and the seashore.

Art Directors, Designers: Why Not Associates, Gordon Young
Photography: Rocco Redondo
Client: Lancaster City Council

⑥⑥ Make design invisible

Peter Wegner, *Blue,* Open Studio CD packaging
Todd Waterbury, Wieden+Kennedy, New York

Wieden+Kennedy Art Director Todd Waterbury frequently collaborates with painter Peter Wegner. Asked by a gallery director to develop what might be called a "Peter Primer," Wegner asked Waterbury to work with him on the project. The final product ended up as a series of thoughts numbered from 1 to 69, each one being a definitive question or declarative idea about Wegner or the world. While reading it, the reader relates each new line to the previous line—each line builds on or subverts the others. Waterbury wanted to show how this pattern leads to a particular way of expanding or contracting the approach that Wegner takes to the world and to his work.

In trying to make the design of the project invisible, Waterbury asked the following questions: Is there a way through language that additional meaning can be given to something that is that simple? Can it be presented in a way that feels more

memorable—that is designed but at the same time doesn't feel like design overwhelms the information?

The first thing Waterbury did was to look at the book as a small piece, all white with black text. The layout sequence is that the first statement appears on the bottom edge of the cover. As the reader turns the page, the first line moves up and its place is taken by the next statement, and so forth, each new statement taking the place of the last, with each preceding one still visible to the reader. Waterbury wanted to express the statements a bit like movie credits, to demonstrate the interrelatedness of each statement, but also its individuality. "It is another way of thinking about narrative. I was thinking about it through the form of a book that made use of the medium but tried to bend it a little bit at the same time."

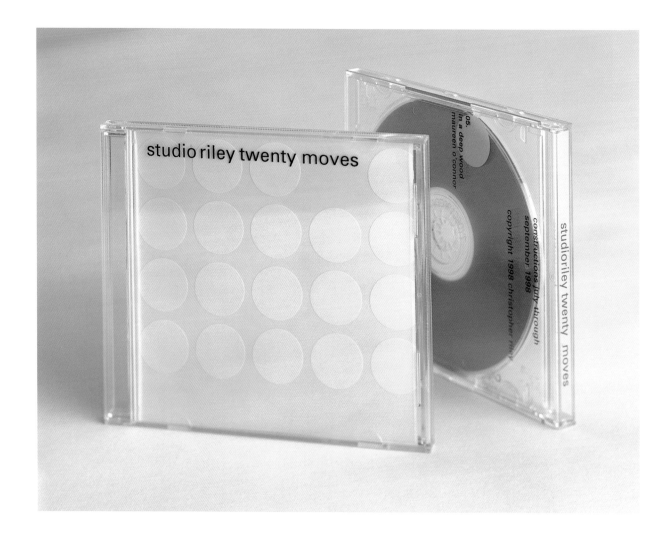

A second example of this kind of "invisible" design is the CD packaging that Waterbury created for a series of recordings entitled *Found*. Russell Davies, the musician who developed the CD, asked friends to record their favorite sounds on cassette tape and then give him the sounds to mix into 16 songs. Waterbury cut a cassette tape in half and sandwiched it between the back of a jewel case and the outer cover. Behind the CD was a gnarled-looking knot of tape. On top was a small bag that contained a booklet with a lost-and-found sticker attached to it. "I tried to make it look like a collection of something you might see blowing in the street, something that had fallen out of someone's wallet or suitcase, that was then reassembled at a lost-and-found department. To me, it understood his intention and executed it in a way that embraced the vernacular, the world of lost and found, but didn't do it in a way that overtook the subject matter," Waterbury notes.

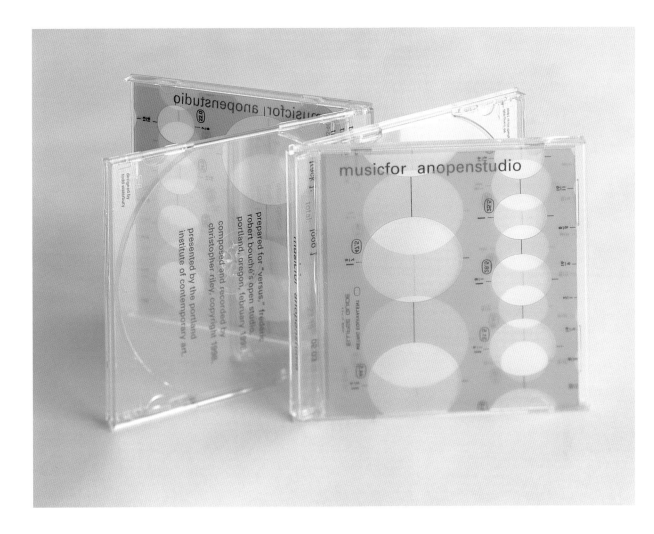

Blue (previous spread)
Art Director, Designer: Todd Waterbury in collaboration with the client
Writing: Peter Wegner
Studio Production: Maria Sabo
Binding: Grossenbacher Brothers
Printing: Jeff Ryan, 21 Steps
Client: Peter Wegner

Studio Riley, Music for an Open Studio CD packaging (above)
Art Director, Designer: Todd Waterbury
Writing: Christopher Riley
Artist, Composer: Christopher Riley

Recognize the limits of digital technology for creative work

Announcement Flyer
Ed Fella

There is a significant disconnect between Ed Fella's teaching and his art. He does not teach the hand-lettering and use of old commercial techniques for which his work is known. "It's not because I don't want to," he notes. "It's just that nobody really wants to learn it. Even my own daughter, who is a graphic designer, never asks me, 'How do you do this lettering?' People want to work with digital technology now. You can't really do anything in the contemporary commercial scene unless you can use the computer to make documents. I can still do what I do because I take my work to a printer, and he scans them in for me, makes the plates. He doesn't even have a camera anymore!"

Ed Fella contends that at 65, he is too old to use a computer. When computers first became readily available over ten years ago, he made a conscious decision not to use one because he didn't really do professional work anymore and, consequently, didn't need it. "I wanted to explore the work I do, and I thought I'd waste a lot of time doing what the next generation is doing." Despite the fact that he doesn't use a computer, his work has had an important impact on designers who have learned from his unorthodox style. "I don't mind it, that history. If you look at

Meggs's *History of Graphic Design*, between "Cranbrook" and "David Carson" is my paragraph. I made a link between that kind of stuff. David Carson went and took it all to the world, whereas in my case it was pretty academic stuff." Ed Fella's work serves as a formal source, which was then adapted by many artists who pushed the boundaries in new media.

When Fella won the Chrysler "Innovation in Design" award (a $10,000 prize), he wanted to do something with the money to improve his technical skills and abilities. He bought himself a video camera but admits to never having actually used it. "I wanted to do some motion stuff, but I never did. My daughter did. I was enticed, but I can't really do it. It's too hard. It's too much effort. I have a hard enough time learning how to do e-mail. I had to hire a student to give me lessons." Although many exciting experiments in font technology were filtered through the unique lens of Ed Fella, he is content to never get himself too involved with technology. He quips sardonically, "Let the next generation do that, make a living doing it. Old guys should get out of the way."

Illustrator, Designer: Ed Fella

click to enter (every day.)

click to enter (raw material is d)

DESIGN FOR THE EVERYDAY

⑥⑧ Let your small shop thrive on high-tech

Web site page, self-promotion card
Worksight

The omnipresence of technology means that even a small shop like Worksight needs a Web site to thrive. Scott Santoro and his partner, Emily, learned to do HTML coding to create their first Web site in 1997. They soon upgraded to Adobe's GoLive web development software and continue to educate themselves about the ins and outs of web technology.

They also own a copy of Flash, which Santoro bought two years ago but has barely even taken out of the box. "I realized I didn't want to learn it because the more Flash-driven sites I see, the more I think they are just driven by the technology," says Santoro. "I realized that in order to use Flash well, I would have to sacrifice a lot of time, and I just wasn't willing to make the commitment. A better idea is to simply hire someone who knows how to make the thing move across and fade off. But then I have to admit that the bells and whistles of Flash are so strong that I wind up trying to figure out how not to make the Web site look like a cliché Flash site. It's a catch-22."

Santoro uses his Web site for all aspects of his small business operations, from marketing to client interaction to portfolio display. In addition, he has many clients in other cities with whom he communicates over the Internet. Although his shop is small, the technological advances of the past few years have made it easier for him to compete effectively in today's business climate.

Designer: Scott Santoro/Worksight

(69) Whatever you think, technology is in control

Xbox broadcast advertising
Miles Murray Sorrell FUEL

Many of the comments made by FUEL about their work remain enigmatic and are, according to the designers, "meant to be subliminal, thought provoking, humorous statements" rather than an obvious description of work habits. In this instance, the sentiment is both paranoid and technophobic, although meant to be read ironically. In its extreme, this sentiment provides a backdrop for a whole intellectual tradition of paranoid techno-phobes and gives an interesting background to the work that FUEL does, which, like most designers, is highly dependent upon technology for its manifestation. The idea of anyone or anything being "in control" is in itself menacing, and yet what exactly technology is in control of, in this instance, is not clear. FUEL provides the designer with a habit of mind rather than a habit of practice, abstracting the everyday relationship to technology in order to gain a new perspective on it.

Designers: Miles Murray Sorrell FUEL
Client: Microsoft Xbox

WHATEVER YOU THINK

TECHNOLOGY

IS IN CONTROL

⑩ Remember that technology serves you; you do not serve technology

Perdu retail space designs
Chase Design Group

The Chase Design Group uses the kinds of machines you would expect to see in a contemporary design office: Macs, a UNIX server, and a token PC. Two staff members serve as tech support. Although there are always issues with technology, at the Chase Design Group the tools are almost always working and always getting better.

In terms of technical disasters, the Chase Design Group has experienced data loss but nothing too dire. "We keep four back-up tape sets in rotation, with the current set backing up continuously and the other sets off-site at two locations. It's hard for us to lose much data. I wouldn't call any tech disaster we've had serious."

Rather than seeking out new technology, Margo Chase is lucky to have people around her who tell her what she needs to know. The Internet has proven to be invaluable to her work as well. "We have a Web site, of course, which is mainly a brochure, and we use the Internet for research and stock photography. We also buy a lot of supplies and other stuff online. Are we too connected? No. E-mail is the best invention ever. Technology is a tool, like a pencil. I use both, every day. Technology only helps unless you're lazy. If you're lazy you deserve what you get."

Designer: Chase Design Group

⑪ Use technology in unexpected ways

Playground in Scotland, in development
Why Not Associates

The same technology that makes it possible for typographers to create new fonts also allows the art of typography to permeate spaces where it might not have previously been an active graphic element.

Why Not is working with frequent collaborator Gordon Young on a Scottish school's new playground. Andy Altmann of Why Not notes, "As you walk into the playground you see a view looking over the fields and mountains toward the sea. What we wanted to do is to put the view into a map on the floor, so as you walk toward this view you walk over what you are seeing—the A-roads, the rivers, and the coastline. There are benches made from the letters that spell out the names of the mountains, such as the Gramkind Mountains. We've done all these things on the floor, and we wanted to go up in the air a bit."

Translating typographic elements into materials such as wood and steel is not a new process, but the consistency provided by computerized fabrication systems makes possibilities that were previously unavailable.

⑦ Work with emerging technologies

Emigre magazine: issue 56 (left), Emigre font catalog (right)
Rudy VanderLans and Zuzana Licko, Emigre

Rudy VaderLans has a utilitarian approach to the use and adoption of technology. When Emigre was started, bitmapped fonts were the only kind of computer font available. FedEx, the Internet, and cell phones didn't exist. VanderLans and Zuzana Licko were still pasting down text galleys with rubber cement. He had never used a computer in his life. When the 128k Mac was first introduced, VanderLans and Licko bought one.

They were challenged to figure out how they could best use this machine with all its shortcomings. There was great resistance to the Macintosh in the design community when it first came out. Designers laughed at them for using it. VanderLans and Licko, with a small group of fellow believers, were among the first to try out this new tool. They hooked a video camera to their Mac to capture low-resolution black-and-white still images and made movies with the first video-editing software. They even sold fonts online before the advent of the World Wide Web, long before anybody else did, using bulletin board software.

When you're out on the edge, you run the risk of becoming too focused on making the technology work, and design and ideas start to take a backseat. VanderLans recalls, "Shortly after PostScript was introduced, we found this guy who was able to hook his Mac to a photo setter, allowing us for the first time ever to output high-resolution fonts onto photographic paper. We would drive over to San Francisco with our files on floppy disks and sit there for hours downloading this stuff, never knowing if it would work."

Calling the new technology "impenetrable and expensive," VanderLans now lets the computer take a backseat in his design work. Although he professes to no longer be "chasing the latest gadgets and software," Emigre continues fuel the imaginations of young designers whose relationship to technology is ever-changing.

Designer: Rudy VanderLans

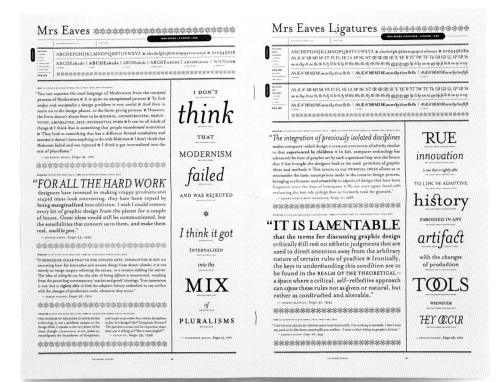

Mrs Eaves · Mrs Eaves Ligatures

Elliott's Fonts

Exocet

Journal

Journal Bold

Journal Small Caps

Keedy Sans

Lunatix

Lo-Res Twenties

Lo-Res Teens

Lo-Res Nines

⑦₃ Make friends with people who know a technology that you want to learn

Blue corporate identity
Why Not Associates

The designers at Why Not have been interested in film from the beginning and have slowly built up a relationship with broadcast technology by teaching themselves how to work in this medium. Why Not does a lot of TV work in-house now, and they have developed a small edit facility—"a studio in a little glass box with a very big Mac and lots of hard drives coming off of it," says Andy Altmann.

Why Not has created corporate identities for several video-editing facilities. Because of this work, they have had a lot of contact with the video and film industry—in fact, one of their clients gave them a screen for their video-editing suite. They weren't scared of trying to do it themselves, but if the money is available on a project, they will go to an edit facility. "They obviously know more about it than we do. We hire an After Effects specialist to help us sometimes. He knows all about broadcast qualities and what is expected."

Close contact with experts in allied fields can not only create practical alliances and impromptu education, but it can also expand the capabilities of your design studio.

Art Directors, Designers: Why Not Associates
Client: Blue Post Production

scott w santoro worksight
46 great jones street
new york new york 10012-1162
graphic design services

t 212.777.3558 • f 212.475.9098
www.worksight.com

(74) Develop an overarching
technology metaphor

Self-promotion cards
Worksight

Scott Santoro of Worksight has developed a metaphor that informs and deepens all the work he does. "I live on a street that has a construction company, a trucking company, a sand-blasting shop, a welder, and a firehouse. It is a very short block and a very active street." The Worksight studio literally sits in a worksite.

Everything that Worksight does derives from an approach that respects the metaphors available to the designer via the industrial world. Worksight's visual language, their point of view, has been a kind of proposition. According to Santoro, plumbing has everything to do with graphic design. "It started out as a joke that I didn't quite believe myself, but the more I looked, the more I found that it would be a great metaphor to use. Plumbing is also my family's trade: my uncles, my father, my cousins—they are all plumbers. I, by contrast, went to art school. Plumbing became a layer, part of my 'everyday' approach that is embedded in there somehow. It is satisfying to have hit upon such an appropriate metaphor, especially one that is flexible enough to allow me to understand design through it."

Santoro uses a pipe connector as an icon, to pique the curiosity of people who view his work. Fragments of an industrial world keep reappearing in his designs. "I find that these lunch boxes, wrenches, and pipes convey an honest beauty, a rugged integrity of purpose. And they can be surprisingly architectural or sculptural. I strive to reveal the beauty in the product, and when a company is proud of who it is and what it makes, then it can afford to be honest and direct. An intrinsic approach is more likely to connect with a diverse audience, which includes not just lawyers, teachers, and students, but also mechanics, carpenters, and plumbers."

Designer: Scott Santoro/Worksight

⑦⑤ It's OK to not go multimedia

Images of America
Worksight

In the current climate of ubiquitous new technology, deciding to stay within a defined realm of graphic design is not an obvious choice. Scott Santoro, whose work reflects a commitment to a basic constructive aesthetic, understands that the bells and whistles of the new media are not all they're cracked up to be.

"I was feeling really bad four or five years ago, because like most graphic designers, I felt that we had missed the boat. Brand-new, 50-person graphic design studios were opening. Students to whom I had just finished teaching graphic design were starting Web firms and within a half-year had 50 people on staff. I was feeling like I just had a little mom-and-pop shop here, and my student, who had just graduated, had a big staff—it just didn't make sense. Then I realized, I just do what I do. I'm not going to turn this technology away, but I will layer it into what I do and not reinvent myself because of the hype."

"I tend to be a traditional graphic designer. I love to do print; I started in that. One of my professors from Pratt, Charles Goslin did a presentation for the AIGA. He said, 'I'm content to be a cobbler, cobbling away in my studio, enjoying the craft of

the thing as well as the thinking. As far as I'm concerned, just cobbling out stuff is fine with me. If I had a shoe store, I'd be cobbling away at the shoes and enjoying the craft of producing nice pieces.' There is a certain self-satisfaction in that. The flow of the craft of graphic design is really nice."

Designer: Scott Santoro/Worksight

⑦⑥ Use the computer as a business tool as well as a creative tool

Web pages
Rudy VanderLans and Zuzana Licko, Emigre

Although Rudy VanderLans and Zuzana Licko were inspired by computer technology when they founded Emigre, they now use technology primarily as a servant for their business. VanderLans comments, "Our Web site is listed in all our catalogs, our magazine, and our ads we run in other magazines. Emigre was selling fonts, magazines, T-shirts, and music long before the Internet and the World Wide Web came about. The Web simply made it easier to sell our products, particularly the fonts. Because they are a digital product—meaning they can be bought and sent out on the Web—roughly 80 to 90 percent of our total sales happen online."

Although VanderLans claims that he is not searching out new technology—or at least not at the rate he used to—he does use the computer daily for his work. "I really like how the PDF format has become the standard for transferring and sharing design files. It has made work flow so much more efficiently. And, of course, as a type foundry, I'm thrilled by the notion that the format allows people to send and share files without sending and sharing the actual font files."

Designer: Zuzana Licko

Personal Growth and Keeping Creativity Alive

77-89

When your body sleeps, your wounds heal and you grow. The state of rest is inherently productive for the physical body—renewal takes place so the wear can begin again. For the designer, the time away from the computer (or notebook) can not only be restorative, but it can also suggest a new way to return. Designers use many diverse strategies to nurture their own creativity and encourage their growth as artists and business people. Reading, relaxing, and getting away from the world of graphic design all play parts in this process.

⑦⑦ Travel as much as possible

1998 *Sphere* magazine
Mark Randall, Worldstudio, Inc.

The Worldstudio Foundation inspires co-founders Mark Randall and David Sterling by providing links to the outside world that are constructive and engaged, which help them to keep their perspectives fresh. Another thing they like to do is travel, and this interest connects with the interests of the Worldstudio Foundation, which, in part, concerns itself with cross-cultural understanding and the introduction of perspective into the work of designers and design students. When Randall travels around the world, he gets to see all kinds of voices that aren't seen in white, Euro-centric design offices. Part of the reason Worldstudio Foundation offers scholarships is to help art and design students who come from minority backgrounds get a leg up in their work and in the industry. These voices make a big difference when they are heard.

Randall prefers the spontaneity of travel as an educational experience to the comparatively staid environment of the design conference. Although such conferences are useful for meeting people, he remarks that in truth the last thing he wants to do is go to a conference about graphic design. He'd much rather go

to a conference of physicists, or some other topic about which he knows little. He's been doing graphic design for over 18 years. "It's not that I know it all," he says. "I just want a little bit more diversity in my life. Not to denigrate conferences, either. I went to the last AIGA conference because they invited me to speak, and I thought it was great. I thought they did a great job, and I saw a lot of really interesting speakers. It wasn't bad, but it is just not a personal interest of mine to go to conferences." Travel allows one to step into a completely unique environment and be bombarded with fresh ideas, sights, and sounds, which is invaluable in any discipline.

Editorial Directors: Mark Randall, David Sterling
Art Directors: Mark Randall, David Sterling
Editor: Peter Hall
Designers: Stefan Hengst, Mark Randall, Klaus Kempenaars, x-Site
Illustrators: Various
Photography: Various
Client: Worldstudio Foundation

⑦⑧ Look at the everyday world for inspiration

Image from Worksight promotional card
Worksight

The idea of staying grounded and connected to the world of the everyday continually infuses the work of Scott Santoro and Worksight. Through the use of the plumbing metaphor, Santoro infuses his work with a practicality and simplicity of language that belies some of the pretentious conceit that the profession of design sometimes exhibits. "My father directs the flow of water. I direct the flow of information. There's a basic similarity between what we both do for a living."

After taking a creative writing course two years ago, Santoro developed his observations into a short story about a backyard clothesline viewed from one of the irregularly shaped windows at the Whitney Museum of Art, part of which is excerpted here and can be read in its entirely on the Worksight Web site.

"...I spoke his dialect from the land of graphic design and knew exactly what he was getting at. Outside, in a neighbor's backyard, sat a poetic example of 'the everyday.' It effortlessly blended life and art, and was as deep as anyone wanted it to be.

"It's a bit of an oxymoron to bring up the philosopher, G. W. F. Hegel, when writing about 'the everyday.' His philosophy's better combined with rocket science. Yet Hegel's maxim should have been flashing above the window, 'The familiar is not necessarily the known.' Of course it would have ruined the refreshing unexpectedness of the moment. The clothesline seemed innocent of any intention other than reeling out a week's worth of freshly washed clothing. But, underneath that layer of utility, it begged the viewer for meaning to be assigned. As Z said, 'It wasn't trying to be anything.' It was nice that way; like a blank canvas—ready, waiting, and full of possibility.

"It's as if the clothesline was metaphorically available for anyone and everyone to pin meaning to it, each viewer as a potential author in a democratic kind of art. The location made sense in the back of the Whitney which touts itself as a museum of American art—clotheslines feel as American as apple pie."

Santoro's observations reflect his intense, daily engagement with the world of the everyday, and the fact that looking carefully at your surroundings can have a significant effect on your art. Letting in the seemingly unimportant and ephemeral can lead to inspiring observations and creative insights into the work of design.

Designer: Scott Santoro/Worksight

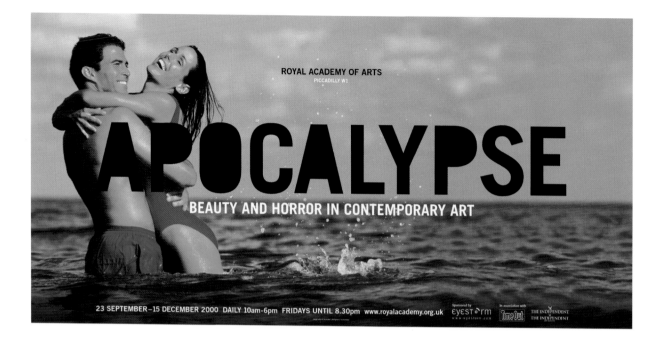

⑦⑨ Watch videos of comedians

Apocalypse poster "Swimmers"
Why Not Associates

To gain a sense of perspective and to get inspiration, Andy Altmann of Why Not Associates watches old English comedy videos. "Morecambe and Wise are probably my favorite. They were a comedy double-act, who modeled themselves originally on Abbott and Costello. They were very British, actually, in the end and became some of the most popular figures of their generation."

Part of his love for British comedy is bound to its surreal nature, which links it to art, such as Lewis Caroll's *Alice in Wonderland*, which makes the regular world look peculiar and the strange seem normal. Typographical experiments, as well as experiments with language and form, created new venues for early 20th-century artists. "Some of these comedians can be quite surreal," Altmann notes. "They make you really look twice at things. This perspective is, in effect, what you want good design to do—make you think about normal things in a strange new way."

Spike Milligan is another comedian that Altmann considers to be not only a pioneering comedian, but also very surreal in his approach. "The surrealist painters so often use humor to make their work effective. It makes sense that surrealism is such an important inspiration to me. Just juxtaposing a word and an image can have such immense power, especially when you least expect it."

Art Directors, Designers: Why Not Associates
Photography: Tim Kivsalaas
Client: The Royal Academy of Arts

Practice and preach, don't theorize and teach

Announcement Flyers
Ed Fella

The work of a commercial graphic designer and the work of a graphic design teacher have very different demands. Nonetheless, these activities share certain elements, and Ed Fella, who has experienced both, has many insights on the subject. After working for over 30 years in Detroit in a large design shop, Fella returned to school at age 48, when he went to Cranbrook to get his master's degree. After graduating, he made his way to Southern California where he taught at Cal Arts for 15 years. He is now retired.

His aphorisms, such as "Rules are taught to be broken only exceptionally" and "Practice and preach, don't theorize and teach," serve as words to the wise as well as pithy summations of his sometimes eccentric approach to design. The precise work of a font designer, for example, is often disrupted in Fella's mostly hand-done lettering experiments. His inimitable style clearly cannot be taught as such, but it can be "preached"—rather than displaying a series of rules to follow, Fella's work and teaching style emphasize courageous creativity. Deeply schooled in the theory of design, he eschews theorization per se in favor of a strong practice and also believes teachers teach best by doing rather than theorizing.

Illustrator, Designer: Ed Fella

⑧¹ Change your environment

Recent posters for Trocadero club, AIGA
Art Chantry

Although Art Chantry is from the Northwest, he moved to St. Louis in 2000. The change of scene provided a drastic change of perspective for Chantry. Often credited as the founder of the graphics style of some major Seattle music movements of the '80s and '90s, such as work for *The Rocket* newspaper, Sub Pop records, and Estrus records, Chantry had a history and identity in Seattle based primarily around subcultural movements. Consequently, when he moved to St. Louis and tried to get jobs outside of the world that he had formed (and that had formed him), it was tricky.

"I moved away from Seattle because I couldn't make a living there anymore," Chantry notes. The economic boom that gripped Seattle in the '90s brought with it both an inflated housing and studio market and a falsely healthy economy demanding design services. Chantry had previously been able

to support himself by teaching and doing design work; in addition, he had a subsidized housing arrangement that he knew would not last. When the bottom fell out in the '90s, things had to change—he needed a change of scene, and he needed to be in an environment that provided more economic stability.

His partner, Jamie Sheehan, also a graphic designer, moved to St. Louis for work, so Chantry turned his back on his entire life and moved from the West to the "Gateway to the West." St. Louis could not be more different from Seattle in terms of culture, economic climate, and social makeup. Designers were paid what Chantry calls "New York rates," and many large corporations were based in St. Louis. All the designers he met worked for large agencies. He found the environment to be very conservative, and there was no alternative culture scene to speak of.

When the market bottomed out in St. Louis, it was like Seattle all over again for Chantry. There was one crucial difference: The weak real estate market in St. Louis had allowed him to purchase a house, which now serves as the home base from which he and Jamie do their freelance work. As a result of his work in Seattle, Chantry feels he is (for better or worse) pigeon-holed into doing work for countercultural products and events such as film festivals, skate parks, and record companies—ironically, none of it originating in St. Louis.

Chantry changed his surroundings and as a result gained a new perspective from the different sights and environments to which he gained access. Although his client base did not change radically, his change of scene helped him get a fresh outlook toward his work.

Designer: Art Chantry

⁸² Have conversations with great talents

Ryuichi Sakamoto, Sampled Life
Hideki Nakajima

Hideki Nakajima derives his primary inspiration from conversations with what he calls "great talents"—people both inside and outside the world of design, particularly musicians, fashion designers, and other artists. According to Nakajima, "The reason I do not go to the bookstore is I know that there is not 'new' creativeness in the strict meaning. It takes at least two or three months to publish a book from the beginning…It is nonsense to find 'new' creativeness in the bookstore. Real 'new' creativeness exists in the brains of great talents."

Nakajima took some photographs for an ongoing series of compositions for *Cut* magazine before he began designing the images utilizing surface, color, and typography. Realizing that he was not a photographer, he turned back to graphic design. In an interview from 1999, he notes, "Through meeting various people such as Ryuichi Sakamoto, Andres Serrano, and Kyoji Takahashi, I realized that the world extends beyond my knowledge and that the outside world is full of extremely talented people. To compete with these people, I had to return to my field, graphic design."

Sometimes, however, great talents can be found at home. For Nakajima, his children are another source of inspiration. He cites "the birth and growth of my babies" as the singular most influential nondesign element that has affected his work. "Sometimes cute expressions I've never done before appear in my design. I used to prefer colorless and strict designs, but I tend to use colorful and soft ones today," he notes.

Creative Directors: Norika-Sky-Sora, Shigeo Goto
Art Director, Designer: Hideki Nakajima
Photography: Mikiya Takimoto
Client: Code

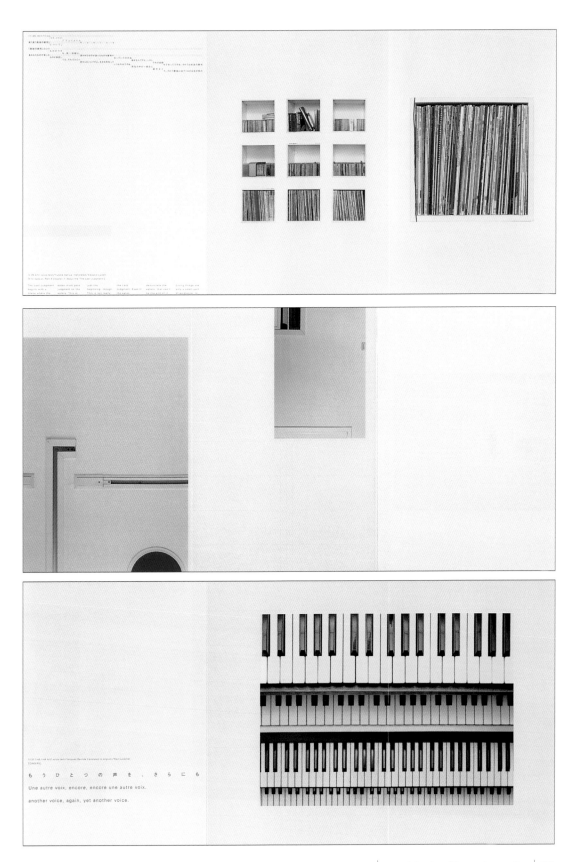

もうひとつの声を、さらにも

Une autre voix, encore, encore une autre voix.

another voice, again, yet another voice.

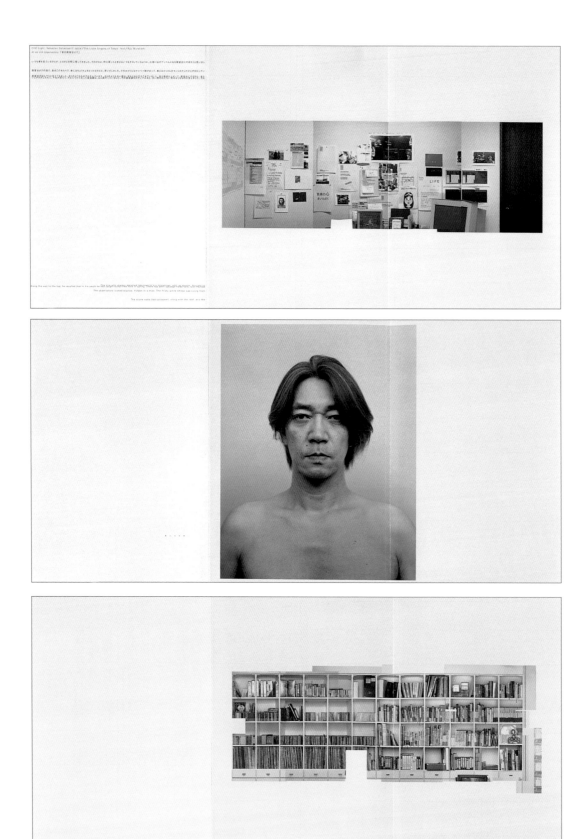

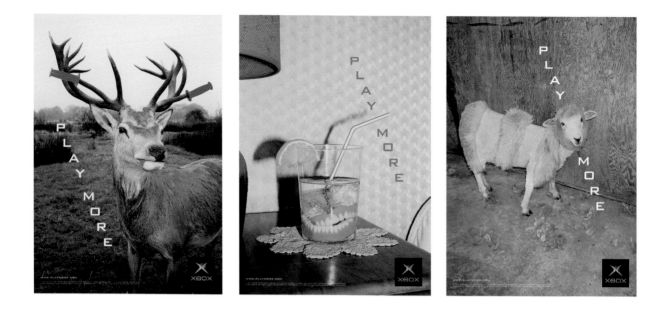

⑧³ Keep creativity alive by any means

Xbox print advertising
Miles Murray Sorrell FUEL

The books *Pure Fuel* and *Fuel 3000* inspired advertising agency creatives at Bartle Bogle Hegarty to commission Miles Murray Sorrell FUEL to create a print campaign for the European launch of Microsoft's new game console Xbox. Damon Murray notes, "We wanted a raw, spontaneous feel to the campaign. The images needed to look as real and natural as possible and the snapshot quality of the pictures helped this. We took all the photographs for the campaign, art-directing ourselves. The design has a strong typographic element, similar to the FUEL books. The Xbox campaign responded to a brief, while at the same time, retained a feeling of our personal work."

Designers, Photographers: Miles Murray Sorrell FUEL
Client: Microsoft Xbox

⑧④ Read a good book

Margo Chase

Margo Chase derives a lot of creative inspiration from reading. "I really love to read, and I spend lots of free time doing it. I read both fiction and nonfiction, as well as that special category of reading that I call 'reading the pictures.' I do most of my reading in bed at night before I go to sleep. Really great writing can cause me to lose sleep and large chunks of my weekend until I've finished.

"My list of favorite books constantly changes based on what I've read most recently. Today's list includes: *Germs, Guns, and Steel: The Fates of Human Societies* by Jared Diamond, *This Is Modern Art* by Matthew Collings, *The Cheese Monkeys: A Novel in Two Semesters* by Chip Kidd, *Possession: A Romance* by A. S. Byatt, and *Liars, Lovers, and Heroes: What the New Brain Science Reveals About How We Become Who We Are* by Steven R. Quartz and Terrence J. Sejnowski.

"I have rather catholic tastes when it comes to books, and, as you might guess, they don't all have direct bearing on my work. A lot of my reading is just decompression and escape. A. S. Byatt's richly romantic writing falls into this category. So does Umberto Eco's *Baudolino*, which I'm currently reading. *Germs, Guns, and Steel* has had some effect on my thinking because it deals with the reasons why some societies are more successful than others. The author suggests that success is based on access to resources rather than on some innate superiority or intelligence. I think he would shudder if he thought I was applying his ideas to success in the design business, but some analogies seem inescapable.

"Chip Kidd's book has more obvious bearing because it's a witty book about design school. *This Is Modern Art* is a wonderfully sardonic and insightful overview of what's happening in modern art these days. Collings's comments and observations keep coming to mind in both positive and negative ways. I've quoted him to my design students more than once.

"As designers we are asked to solve all kinds of different problems, yet our own experiences are often too limited to provide us with the insights or understanding to do this well. I think the part of my brain that intuitively 'gets it' is the part that has unconsciously absorbed the ideas and concepts put forth in books.

"Reading is an extremely important part of my life, and I can't imagine what it's like for those who don't enjoy it. At the very least, it broadens my horizons and makes for interesting conversation at the dinner table!"

体力がある女

やせてない

⑧⑤ Set up shop in a foreign country during a recession

Nike Swim print advertising
John C Jay, Wieden+Kennedy, Tokyo

The Wieden+Kennedy office has grown into a shop of 47 staff members, mostly Japanese, who work with some of the most important and influential Japanese brands.

When Wieden+Kennedy first decided to open the shop, Japan was in the middle of a decade-long recession, and the Japanese economy was in shambles. Advertising expenditures around the world were down, and many observers considered opening a new Japanese office as a great risk. Jay notes, "From a business standpoint, if you read the *Wall Street Journal* or the business pages of the *New York Times*, one would think it would be economic suicide to come over here and open a new business, but we felt that anytime there is a long economic recession, cultural changes are bound to occur."

At times like this, unique business opportunities arise. Jay explains, "That was what we focused on, that's what we held as

our faith. And, of course, we were aiming to reach the youth culture that we knew was very powerful. But it isn't until the moment you truly get inside it yourself, really immerse yourself culturally, that you begin to understand how influential Japanese youth culture is to the rest of us in the creative world."

Wieden+Kennedy opened with only one client, but fortunately it was an enormous one: the Japanese arm of the company that grew up with the Portland office, Nike. Jay comments, "My goal was not to be a typical agency. Even within the Wieden world, we wanted to do something different. We wanted to come in and become firmly entrenched in the cultural landscape of Japan. We did not want to be an office that depended on Western clients for their leftovers, their small adaptation projects. We wanted to work with the best and the brightest of the leaders here in Japan, people who were looking for innovation, who were looking for change, and who were looking for the highest

丈夫な女

'美しい女'の答え方が、
少し変わってきていると思う。
ナイキスイムウエア、誕生。

食欲がある女

'美しい女'の見え方が、
少し変わってきていると思う。
ナイキスイムウエア、誕生。

levels of strategic and creative execution. Getting our message across—you can only prove that point by doing work."

Taking the risk to open a new shop in Japan was based on Jay's confidence that he could find a staff that could partner with him and grow the company into a dynamic entity and into one of the leading ad firms in Japan. In addition, he saw the economic and cultural climate in Japan as ripe for change and for dramatic challenge to the status quo.

Creative Directors: John C Jay, Sumiko Sato
Art Director: Nagi Noda
Copywriter: Sumiko Sato
Photography: Shoji Uchida
Production Coordinator: Sun AD
Client: Nike Japan

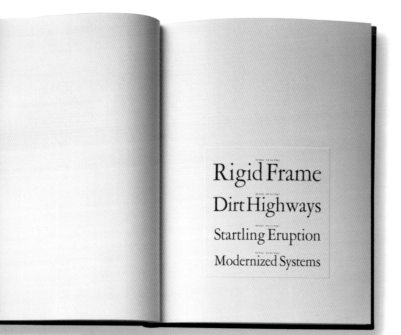

Rigid Frame

Dirt Highways

Startling Eruption

Modernized Systems

⑧⑥ Work with visual artists

Peter Wegner, *American Types*
Todd Waterbury, Wieden+Kennedy, New York

For a number of years, Todd Waterbury of Wieden+Kennedy has been collaborating with visual artist Peter Wegner, whose work deals with the relationships between social conventions and formal artistic elements such as color.

The artist, who usually shows his work in galleries, wanted to work with Waterbury to express his ideas in a book. The artist's work tends to be very large pieces of plywood—8 feet x 10 feet (2.4 m x 3 m)—at their largest. Rather than create a record of a particular show, Wegner wanted to explore and collaborate with another artist to see his vision in a different medium. Together, Waterbury and Wegner worked with the form of the book to translate the art into something more intimate. Although Waterbury had not designed a book before, he and Wegner share a similar aesthetic, as well as a love of ephemera. Their collaboration pushes the limits of the book form to create an experience that they hoped would be more memorable for the reader.

The process of collaboration was somewhat informal. Wegner had developed a body of work over a number of years. During that time, he would ask a few friends, including Waterbury, into his studio to discuss the work. This experience gave Waterbury insight into the process of the paintings, both how they were done and how the thinking behind them had developed.

The work that Waterbury does with Wegner is different from his work at Wieden+Kennedy because the collaborative nature of the project eliminates the idea of "creative" and "client." Because the relationship is not commercial in nature, Waterbury can try work that proceeds at a very different pace, with different aims. The ideas and sometimes complex execution provide an outlet for Waterbury to conceptualize the work of design outside of the commercial realm.

Art Director, Designer: Todd Waterbury in collaboration with the artist
Writing: Peter Wegner
Studio Production, Book Production: The Felt Hat
Photography: Peter Wegner
Printing: Jeff Ryan, 21 Steps
Binding: Grossenbacher Brothers
Client: Peter Wegner

THINGS TO do
before I die

☑ OPEN & RUN A DESIGN
STUDIO IN NEW YORK
☑ HAVE SEX WITH 2 WOMEN
☑ KEEP CLOSE CONTACT
with Mom IN AUSTRIA
☑ find a GREAT girlfriend
☐ WORK A YEAR OR TWO WITHOUT
CLIENTS, DESIGN EXPERIMENTS ONLY
☐ DRIVE a TRUCK THROUGH SIBERIA
☐ MOVE TO SRI-LANKA
☐ Touch SOMEBODY'S
HEART with GRAPHIC Design

⑧⑦ Take some time off

To-do list
Stefan Sagmeister

The year before Stefan Sagmeister took time off from client work had been the most successful to date. Business was flowing in, and the then-booming economy had filled their coffers. In addition, the small firm had won many important awards; Sagmeister had gained an international reputation and was invited to speak all over the world.

The only problem—Sagmeister was bored. The work had become repetitive, and the client demands stifled his flame of creativity. When he was invited to Cranbrook to give a work-shop, he observed the students' work and lifestyle. "I actually got rather jealous of all the mature students there being able to spend their entire day just experimenting," says Sagmeister "Then Ed Fella came into the studio and showed me all the notebooks with his freewheeling typographic experiments. That did it. I settled on a date a year in advance, and I called up all my clients."

Sagmeister tried to fill that year with happy experiments. "My work during that time can be summed up by a list of all the things that I felt would be worthwhile exploring but never had

the time. This included things as simple as thinking about the whole wide world and my place within it, all the way to more concrete projects, like designing fictitious CD covers under time pressure—doing them in three hours rather than my customary three months—and seeing how that self-imposed restriction changes the process and the result."

Sagmeister spent his time developing a number of what he calls "seed projects" for future collaborations with clients. He comments, "Because my brain has a tendency to follow the well-beaten path, I thought it might be helpful to start a project not from within itself but from an outside departure point, again with the hope of arriving at a different solution."

Although he claims that the results of his sabbatical are not yet clear, Sagmeister has learned to approach his design work with a new enthusiasm. "In any case, I got my love for design back, so it was definitely worth it."

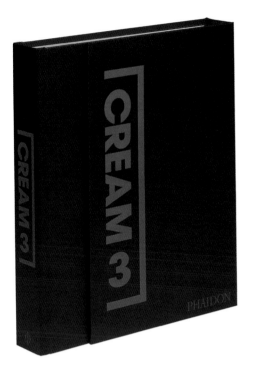

⑧⑧ Develop personal growth and personal taste; you are what you eat

Cream 3 cover and spreads
Miles Murray Sorrell FUEL

Phaidon asked FUEL to design a 448-page art book after seeing *Fuel 3000* and the work they had done for White Cube. The books represents a major collection of work from 100 contemporary artists from around the world. It was a challenge for the firm to design a template for such an extensive collection of work that retained variety and interest while keeping a necessary order and consistency. It is the first book of this kind that FUEL has designed. The double cover folds over with a magnetic fastening. The opportunity to work with art from some of the world's most renowned artists in the design of this book gave FUEL access to a steady diet of their peers: both nourishing and challenging.

Designers: Miles Murray Sorrell FUEL

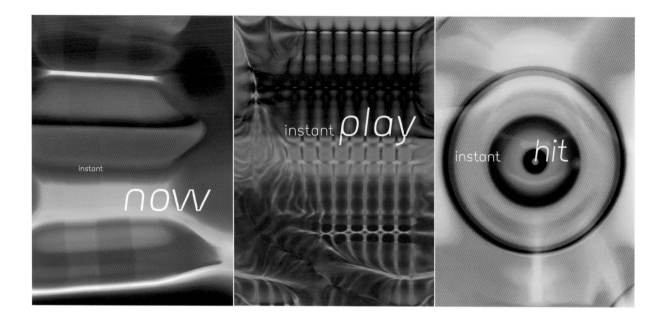

instant now

instant play

instant hit

⑧⑨ Take risks with your career

Presto 3: "Instant Go"
John C Jay, Wieden+Kennedy, Tokyo

John C Jay spent most of his career in New York City. He started in editorial design, gaining both experience in and reverence for both making magazines and collecting news. He worked with a variety of editors and writers, all the while learning how to tell important stories through visuals and words.

Then Jay moved into the field of fashion where, he observes, "many times words are not evident or necessary." He served as long-time creative director and then marketing director for Bloomingdale's in New York, back in the day when stores like that were important icons in the cultural (and not simply the retail) world. He cites his training in what he calls "cultural authenticity" to be the most important aspect of the editorial work that he brought into the fashion field. "Then, after 13 years, it seems to be in our nature to challenge our clients, to tell them they are not taking enough risks, that they are not looking at the big picture. What happens is that creative people themselves become a victim of this, become too immersed in their tiny little businesses and lose sight of the bigger picture. Creative people tend to lose the ability to take risks."

In 1993 Jay left New York, not for his former haunts of Paris, Milan, or Berlin, but for Portland, Oregon. His move to Portland to work for ad giant Wieden+Kennedy was a risky one. He explains, "That was my first radical step in finding a way to not become too comfortable with myself, my career, and what I wanted to do creatively."

Looking for some way to shake up "my own status quo," in 1998, Jay moved across the Pacific Ocean to open the Tokyo office of Wieden+Kennedy. Tokyo offered Jay a unique opportunity to take the culture and values of Wieden+Kennedy to one of the most exciting cities in the world, a city that contains the most influential youth and pop culture. "I wanted to apply some of our thinking, be a sponge, soak it up, and see if we couldn't spread some of that learning through our network around the world."

Jay's approach to challenging himself permeates his work as well. The Presto 3 campaign was consciously created to avoid commercial conventions, and to inspire physical movement viscerally, through the movement of sound and visuals, without the image of an athlete or traditonal sport. Three types of "movement" were featured: the music of electronica, hip hop orchestra, and human beat box. The goal was to illustrate that the Presto concept had grown to another level.

Creative Directors: John C Jay, Sumiko Sato
Art Director: Eric Cruz
Copywriter: Barton Corley
Client: Nike Asia

90-100

Partnerships and Strategic Synergie

Designers are consistently engaging in collective work and partnering with people with different skills and interests to see their ideas through to fruition. Sometimes this collaboration can manifest in the sharing of technical skills—working with an engineer to program a Web site, for example—and sometimes can constitute sharing ideas with people in other fields of expertise. Whether it is a printer, a creative team, or a friend who does something totally different but needs a poster, all of these relationships can constitute partnerships. They can expand skills and reignite interest in design. They can open up designers to new fields and new clients and inspire creation in different media.

The contemporary era of design is an era of consolidation, mergers, and acquisitions in the commercial art field. Design firms now need to be more flexible and open to partnerships. More specialized firms—and even solo designers—exist than ever before. More and more it is the norm for clients to have multiple firms working for them. For example, the Web design might be handled by one firm, and advertising by another, design and publicity by still others. Because so much work is outsourced, designers must learn to be adaptable and to work with many other people as they complete projects.

Collaboration may not always be a matter of choice, but a matter of necessity.

⑨⁰ The secret of a successful partnership is to never compromise

Märchenstüberl JUERGEN TELLER

Jürgen Teller books
Miles Murray Sorrell FUEL

The designers at FUEL have a strong working relationship. "Good ideas are formed without compromise," comments Damon Murray. "Equally good work is made easier if it is produced with like-minded creatives, such as the photographer Jürgen Teller. With him there is an element of trust and mutual respect. The best work is made by and for people who are not prepared to compromise."

Miles Murray Sorrell FUEL has known and worked with Jürgen Teller for over ten years. Initially the team had asked him to shoot a portrait of themselves in their studio for one of their magazines, *Grey*. The relationship grew when Teller asked FUEL to design an exhibition of his work at his house. FUEL then went on to design his show at the Photographers' Gallery in London and, from that project, other exhibitions across Europe and in New York. Throughout this period, FUEL also designed books and catalogs to accompany Teller's personal work.

For FUEL, never compromising means making choices early in the creative process, which assures that all participants are in agreement in terms of the parameters of the project. Although "like-minded" is a vague descriptor, when finding creative partners, FUEL insists they know it when they see it.

Designers: Miles Murray Sorrell FUEL
Photography: Jürgen Teller

⑨¹ Collaborate with someone in a different field

Lou Reed video
Stefan Sagmeister

Stefan Sagmeister co-directed a Lou Reed music video with Robert Peijo, a documentary filmmaker. Before working on this project, Sagmeister had no experience with moving pictures whatsoever. Because of his inexperience, he asked his friend for help—Peijo had much more experience with being on the set, directing a crew properly, and with postproduction. Sagmeister had worked directly with Reed before, designing the CD art for the 2001 release, *Ecstasy*, so he was comfortable with ensuring that the concepts that he suggested were clear with Lou and with the record label.

Sagmeister enjoys the medium of music video but has not gone out to try to get more jobs in the field because he does not really like the MTV format. He says, "I don't think we would design CDs if we hated record stores. And that might all change soon, with broadband coming. Chances are pretty high that the main delivery mechanism for a music video will not be

MTV anymore but the Web, and then it is a new situation. Bands that have tiny budgets will be able to make videos, which will allow for a lot of freedom."

Sagmeister has gained new knowledge in the field of video design and production, an experience that will help him explore new technologies of the Internet, as well as open up imaginative processes that suggest new ways of doing design.

Directors: Stefan Sagmeister, Robert Peijo

⅏ Collaborate with someone whose skills complement your own

St. Louis Film Fest poster
Art Chantry

Jamie Sheehan's skills complement Art Chantry's in a dramatic way. They have been working together since 1994, and now share a studio (and a house) in St. Louis. Sheehan is adept at computer technology, whereas Chantry is self-admittedly not, instead taking a sociocultural approach to their usefulness. "Computers," says Chantry, "especially in their early days, were a process in erasing localized culture. And because culture is what I am interested in, it was a choice not to work with them. As it has developed it is now where underground subculture exists."

Chantry describes Sheehan as a "crack typographer" and himself as a "lettering artist," complementary and yet very different skills. Sheehan has had a lot of experience in copy writing and thinking up gimmicks, whereas Art's work is primarily the creation and promotion of a specific style.

Art Chantry's involvement in the do-it-yourself punk scene in the 1980s and '90s in the Pacific Northwest created the context for his distinctive style and the reach of his work. The graphic elements of such a scene are limited but distinct—record and CD packaging, event posters, and weekly newspaper design all fueled Chantry's success as a pioneering designer in this particular milieu.

Designers: Art Chantry, Jamie Sheehan

Collaboration does not depend on compromise but rather on good decisions about whom you work with

Emigre magazine, issue 24, posters, *Supermarket* book cover
Rudy VanderLans and Zuzana Licko, Emigre

Although the content of *Emigre* magazine could not exist without a number of creative contributors, editor Rudy VanderLans keeps a close eye on the collaborative details. "The content of *Emigre* is determined by me," says VanderLans. "I invite people to contribute. They submit the work. Sometimes the work they submit is perfect, and we publish it nearly as is. Other times the contributors need input and feedback, and I give them my opinion."

VanderLans has worked with some of the best type and editorial designers in the world. In addition, by keeping his contributor list broad, he has established groundbreaking conversations between designers, visual artists, musicians, and writers. What makes it work? VanderLans explains, "The trick is to let people do what they enjoy doing and what they're good at, which is often the same thing. The success of any collaboration, I imagine, lies not so much in the willingness to compromise but in who you select to work with."

Designer: Rudy VanderLans

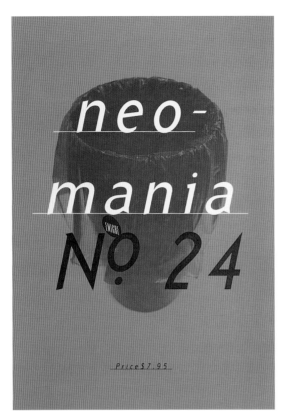

neo-
mania

EMIGRE

№ 24

Price $7.95

[DRAMATIZATION]

2

PLEASE, DO NOT ATTEMPT
THIS AT HOME

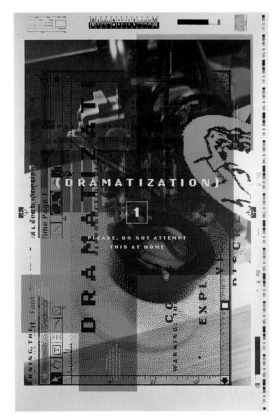

[DRAMATIZATION]

1

PLEASE, DO NOT ATTEMPT
THIS AT HOME

SUPERMARKET

NOTES ON THE MOJAVE DESERT. WORDS AND IMAGES BY RUDY VANDERLANS. A GINGKO PRESS BOOK.

⑨⁴ Find a mutually beneficial relationship

Sphere magazine, tolerance issue
Mark Randall, Worldstudio Foundation

After the debacle of the last issue of *Sphere* magazine (it was slated to come out on 9/11/01 and it featured some highly critical political images and rhetoric), Adobe showed interest in working on the issue of *Sphere* that was slated to come out in February 2003. Adobe identifies strongly with what the magazine represents and wanted to participate in the process of its creation. Adobe was content to stay out of the editorial end but merged their interests with Worldstudio Foundation by supplying five Adobe Achievement Award winners. These young designers, together with five Worldstudio Foundation Scholarship winners, were paired with graphic designers, including Michael Beruit at Pentagram and Karen Fong at Imaginary Forces. The teams created posters on the theme of tolerance, which formed the centerpiece of the magazine. The editorial content around these posters talked about how artists and designers deal broadly with the theme of tolerance in their work.

From a practical standpoint, it was the first time that Worldstudio, Inc. received money to actually design the magazine. Adobe is underwriting the editorial costs and a large portion of the printing costs. Adobe benefits from this partnership by reaching a highly qualified audience for their product, InDesign. A component of the project is that all the studios have to learn InDesign, and the entire publication has to be created using InDesign. It supports the ideals of the foundation, it gets the message out to over 15,000 people, and it engages the creative community in a pro-social project—posters about tolerance. In addition, this issue will be distributed to schools and colleges as well as constituencies of the Southern Poverty Law Center.

2003 Sphere magazine
Editorial and Creative Directors: Mark Randall, David Sterling
Design: Daniela Koenn
Editors: Peter Hall, Emmy Kondo
Illustration, Photography: Various
Client: Worldstudio Foundation

worldstudio foundation

Born of the conviction that creativity holds enormous power for social change, Worldstudio Foundation nurtures a pro-active studio of tomorrow through its scholarship programs, mentorship initiatives and publications.

Putting its ideals into action, Worldstudio Foundation's college scholarship program is tailored specifically to increase diversity in the design/arts professions, and to encourage students to use their talents to give back to their communities. The Foundation's "Help Kids Create" mentoring program pairs at-risk teens with creative professionals to shape socially relevant public messages. Finally, the publication you are reading – *Sphere* – was designed to actively engage the creative community in the issues that challenge us today.

create! don't hate. tolerance poster project

The idea of publishing a variety of posters with a common cause

SUPPORT VARIETY

NIKESPHERE.COM   SWOOSH

⑨⑤ Allow each creative team to determine its collaborative approach

Nike Apparel print advertising
Todd Waterbury, Wieden+Kennedy, New York

Todd Waterbury of Wieden+Kennedy works with a writer as a creative partner for most of his Wieden+Kennedy projects. He finds that the approach to collaboration in such a situation comes primarily from the creative team rather than being dictated by the project. He comments, "Sometimes a writing partner who is completely opposite in viewpoint and style works, because it creates conflict and forces commitment and clarity on what the solutions can be. This is based, though, on the approach that both work as individuals first and then come together to present, discuss, argue, rebuild, and so on." At other times, however, the writer is the other side of the same conceptual coin and the collaboration is more of a deepening of sensibilities. This situation arises less frequently, but when it does occur, Waterbury finds that the results yield work that satisfies on a number of levels.

Art Director: Storm Tharp
Copywriter: Jonathan Cude
Creative Director: Todd Waterbury
Executive Creative Director: Dan Wieden
Studio Artist: Jan Meyer
Photography: Liz Collins
Client: Nike

⁹⁶ Take a risk in choosing collaborative partners

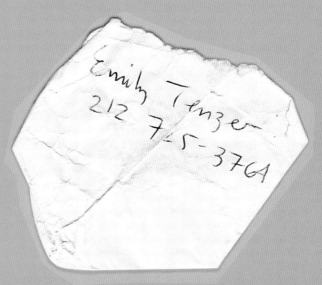

The number she gave
Worksight Studio

Scott and Emily Santoro are co-principals of Worksight, which they founded. Scott had worked at Landor Associates, where he developed visual identities for national brands, and at Mobil Oil Corporation, where he held the position of senior designer in charge of internal communications. In 1986, he returned to school to earn a master's in graphic design.

"I was looking for office space in a typesetting shop where Emily was the office manager. I immediately began dating her and at the same time began forming my company. I asked her if she would like to help out with a project, which led to another, and eventually she wanted to leave her existing job and join me at Worksight. It was a big risk—there is probably some rule out there that states that one should never ask his/her date to help form a business together, but we knew that we were interested in each other."

Scott does the heavy lifting in design, and Emily manages the complex production of books and catalogs. Scott comments that Emily's training in a field outside of design makes her an ideal sounding board. "She brings another set of coordinates to the mix of graphic design and isn't tied down to any of the rules that we all learned. There's a kind of everyday smartness to her responses that affects all of the design work we create."

Although creating such a partnership involves taking a great risk, the benefits of their collaboration and creative partnership have kept the couple in business for over 12 years. They push each other to new intellectual and creative endeavors, and their work is better because of their partnership.

UTOPIA

THIS IS THE 5TH IN A SERIES OF TEN.
ART CHANTRY
EXAMINES WORKPLACE FLEXIBILITY
FROM THE PERSPECTIVE OF
THE FOUNDER AND FORMER CEO
OF THE RECORD COMPANY SUB POP.
THE RESULTS? CHANGE
THE DULL ROUTINE OR SELL OUT.
UTOPIA IS A NEW COATED
LINE FROM APPLETON PAPERS.
ART'S ISSUE IS PRINTED ON UTOPIA
TWO, BLUE WHITE DULL,
100LB. TEXT.

IDEALLY, MOBILITY WITHIN THE WORKWORLD WILL RESTRUCTURE FAMILY & COMMUNITY. NO LONGER WILL PARENTS ONLY SEE THEIR CHILDREN AS THEY PUT THEM TO BED. WORK & PLAY WILL BECOME INTEGRATED, AS OUR DAY BECOMES RICHER & MORE COMPLEX.

...AND IF WORK BECOMES TOO BORING, YOU CAN **SELL OUT** AND **BLOW IT OFF** ALTOGETHER.

⁹⁷ Partner with companies willing to take risks

Appleton Paper Utopia promotions
Art Chantry

The Appleton piece was part of a larger project for which
Chantry had been hired. Appleton created an advisory design
council, which was tasked with giving feedback to them on their
new Utopia paper line. Part of the job was for each member
of the design council to produce a piece as a part of a series.
Each member was to interview a person of a certain societal
niche—anyone from a prisoner to a CEO—and ask the person
to define the word *utopia*. The designers would then create a
piece (within restricted specs) on Utopia papers presenting this
personal vision. Sumata thought it would be funny to assign
Chantry a CEO, so he chose Bruce Pavitt of the independent
record label Sub Pop. Chantry notes, "This pointed out that
'CEO' can mean a lot of different things."

Designer: Art Chantry

PART 1

The Inspiration

TERN was born out of the Council's determination to make the most of Government grant support and to weave into rebuilt sea front areas and new private sector developments a unique personality that would endure, make sense to a wide public and bring delight in it's obvious originality and imagination.

THE INSPIRATION

Morecambe Bay is a rich ecosystem and a bird habitat of international importance. It is the most important wintering site in the UK for dunlin, oyster catcher, curlew and turnstone and has a dependant population of more than 285,000 wildfowl and wading birds.

The bird life of Morecambe Bay is the inspiration for TERN.

POTENTIAL

TERN has brought sculpture and artist designed pavement games and street furniture to the initial phases of reconstruction. It has captured the hearts and minds of the local community and set Morecambe apart from its past and its competitors. TERN has won the design award of the Lancaster Civic Society and gained national recognition last year, as winner of the Arts Council's, Working for Cities Award in the Arts in Progress category.

TERN has the potential to;

expand outwards along Morecambe's seafront to the edge of the built up area and beyond;

create a very special signature on England's north west coastline;

transform a fading seaside resort into a proud town and a contemporary visitor destination; and

bring public art to large numbers of people.

To realise this exceptional potential TERN must continue to influence the rebuilding process in Morecambe, master plan by master plan, phase by phase and contract by contract over the entire rebuilding period, to 2001. To do so it must secure exceptional capital funding on a scale provided only through the Arts Council Lottery Fund.

TERN
The Arts led Regeneration project on Morecambe Bay
Lancaster City Council December 1996

⑨⑧ Partner with civic organizations

Tern proposal document
Why Not Associates

Because Why Not has worked on so many public art projects, they have grown to understand the process of proposing and following through with projects that have very different audiences from their commercial work. The audiences for the public artwork are often in a different position than an audience for commercial work—they do not need to be convinced of anything, they do not need to be sold anything, and the information they are gaining by seeing a piece is often both highly involved in the form and not particularly essential.

On the other hand, partnering with civic organizations to produce public art requires that the concept of the audience remain broad. Although the pieces need not appeal to everyone, they generally should not offend, either. In the pavement for the Tern project, for example, Why Not needed to come up with words related to birds. They chose to use quotations from a range of authors—not just Shakespeare and Milton. They chose to use

vernacular language as well as literary language so that their work could be as comprehensible to as many people as possible.

Partnering with civic organizations to create public art puts the designer in touch with broader audiences than they would normally reach. The concerns of the public and their elected representatives must be respected and acknowledged in the process of design, which is something designers rarely have to consider in their work otherwise.

Art Directors, Designers: Why Not Associates
Client: Lancaster City Council

Forge partnerships that broaden your cultural horizons

Lingerie Perdu
Chase Design Group

Developing a lingerie store for a client in Jeddah, Saudi Arabia, tested the partnering abilities of the Chase Design Group, but it provided an effective outcome. When Chase Design Group was asked, before 9/11, to work with Ehab Mashat, they had before them the opportunity to create a context for the lingerie market that had never been known in the Middle East. Mashat's family had been selling lingerie in Saudi Arabia's bazaars for three generations, and Mashat had the radical vision of elevating lingerie from an under-the-counter commodity to the status of socially acceptable apparel.

Events of 9/11 resulted in strained relations between the United States and many Middle Eastern countries, but the partnership between Chase Design Group and Mashat remained strong. The first store was opened to great acclaim, and the second store will be opening in 2003. The goal of the stores is to create a venue where Saudi women can get what they want: beautiful lingerie in a fashionable store that rivals designer boutiques abroad.

Partnering with Los Angeles–based Chase Design Group proved a good match for this new company. Chase Design Group was involved in every aspect of the project, from choosing the name, creating the interior, specifying the fixtures, producing the signage, and designing the mannequins. Chase successfully created a branding strategy that adhered to the fundamentals of Islam and Saudi culture, while also meeting the modern business objectives of the client.

The largest problem was conceptual: how does one brand a lingerie store in a country where photos of sexy women cannot be used? Or even any shape of a woman? The Chase Design Group's solution is both effective and elegant. Starting with the development of a bilingual font and working with the tradition of sensual poetry in the Arabic tradition, calligraphic form played an enormous role in the solution to the Perdu brand identity. Suggestive texts and colors created a feeling of warm sensuality that became the core of the brand and identity while successfully avoiding the cultural restrictions. The client provided a challenging and exciting project for the Chase Design Group, and the designers provided just the right amount of Western marketing expertise and style to make the brand really stand out in Saudi Arabia.

Art Director: Margo Chase
Designers: Margo Chase, Patricia Guerra
Project Manager: Husam Khalil
Photography: Husam Khalil
Client: Ehab Mashat

The Hispanic sector is the fastest growing demographic in the U.S., a marketer's dream. Hate crimes targeting Hispanics and Central and South American immigrants continue to rise. Tolerance is more than economics.

⑩ Help other people collaborate

Create! Don't Hate: Campaign for Tolerance
Worldstudio Foundation

Part of the Worldstudio Foundation's mission is to help young designers find mentors as they move from their school years and into their professional lives. The idea of publishing a variety of posters with a common cause initially came out of the Worldstudio Foundation's ongoing "Create! Don't Hate: Campaign for Tolerance" mentoring initiative. The plan was to set up a mentoring program that paired design and illustration students with high-profile designers to develop the posters.

The mentoring aspect of the poster project was particularly successful. Essential design elements, such as information, experience, knowledge, and ideas, flowed back and forth, making the process valuable to both designers and students. Eleven teams took part, and the whole operation was funded in part by Adobe, who also provided the InDesign application for the creation of the pieces.

Although collaboration has always been a part of the way that the Worldstudio Foundation partners David Sterling and Mark Randall have worked, providing an opportunity for young people and more experienced designers to get together on a project with a high degree of social relevance was particularly rewarding.

Designers: Jim Stringer, The Art Institute of Atlanta (left), Jenny Tran, Art Center (right)
Mentors: Bill Grant, Grant Design (left), Karin Fong, Imaginary Forces (right)
Client: Worldstudio Foundation

INTOLERANCE DESTROYS THE FABRIC OF AMERICA

ALL QUOTES WERE FOUND ON INTERNET MESSAGE BOARDS OF MAINSTREAM SITES SUCH AS YAHOO, MSN.COM AND THE WASHINGTON POST

About the contributors

Andy Altman, Why Not Associates
Andy Altmann and David Ellis are the brains of Why Not Associates, a 15-year-old firm that has left its mark across a wide swath of projects in the United Kingdom and beyond. Their unorthodox style of working, their varied client list, and their experimentation in a variety of media give their work a distinct—but never predictable—look. Their monograph, *Why Not*, was published by Booth-Clibborn Editions.

Why Not Associates
22c Shepherdess Walk
London N1 7LB UK
t. 0207.253.2244
f. 0207.253.2299
www.whynotassociates.com

Art Chantry, Art Chantry Design
Art Chantry began his life as a designer in the Seattle area, where he worked with musicians and record labels in developing a signature style for the grunge movement of the 1990s. He was art director of the alternative weekly, *The Rocket*, and also developed a body of work for Seattle independent record label, Sub Pop. He has recently relocated to St. Louis, where he continues to work as a freelancer. His monograph *Some People Can't Surf* (2001) is available from Chronicle Press.

Art Chantry Design Co.
P. O. Box 63275
St. Louis, MO 63163 USA
t. 314.773.9421
f. 314.773.3295

Margo Chase, Chase Design Group
Margo Chase founded the Chase Design Group 15 years ago. Noted early on for designing hundreds of logos and identities for clients such as Madonna, Cher, and *Buffy the Vampire Slayer*, the company is now equally well known for corporate identities, packaging and product design, motion graphics, advertising, and interior design. Widely recognized by many awards and accolades, Margo Chase was originally trained to be a veterinarian.

Chase Design Group
2255 Bancroft Ave.
Los Angeles, CA 90039 USA
t. 323.668.1055
f. 323.668.2470
www.chasedesigngroup.com

Ed Fella
Ed Fella worked as a commercial designer for 30 years in Detroit before he went back to school at age 48 to get his M.F.A. at Cranbrook. He retired from Cal Arts after teaching there for 13 years. He still participates in the graduate classes and continues to pursue his "art practice." His work is shown widely, and his book of photographs, *Edward Fella: Letters on America* (2000), was published by Princeton Architectural Press.

Ed Fella
California Institute of Arts
Valencia, CA 91355 USA
t. 661.255.1050 ext. 2621
f. 661.259.5871

John C Jay, Wieden+Kennedy, Tokyo
John C Jay is a partner of Wieden+Kennedy, which has offices in New York, London, Amsterdam, Tokyo, and Portland, Oregon, and is also co-executive creative director for Wieden+Kennedy, Tokyo. Jay previously served as executive vice president of marketing and creative director for Bloomingdale's in New York. Jay was chosen by *American Photographer* magazine as one of the "80 Most Influential People in Photography." He received the Gold Medal at the Leipzig Bookfair in 1998 for the book, *Soul of the Game*. He has received multiple awards for interior design, publication design, graphics, photography, short film, packaging design, and advertising, including gold and silver medals from the NY Art Directors Club and The One Show in New York. Examples of Jay's work have also appeared in a variety of museum and gallery exhibitions including Museum of Modern Art, New York (film and video); Victoria & Albert, London; Cooper-Hewitt Museum, New York; the Pompidou Museum, Paris; The Field Museum, Chicago; and International Center of Photography, New York.

Jay's independent company, Studio J, has served as creative consultant for the international marketing of *Star Wars* Episodes 1 and 2 and worked with director Oliver Stone on the marketing of *U-Turn*. Jay has served on the International Advisory Committee for the Wexner Center for the Arts, is a founding member of the Board of Directors of P.I.C.A. (Portland Institute of Contemporary Art), and a member of the Board for Camp Caldera, a nonprofit art and ecology center in Oregon.

John C Jay
Wieden+Kennedy
7-5-6 Roppongi Minatoku
Tokyo Japan 106-0032
t. 81.3.5771.2900
f. 81.3.5771.2712
www.wk.com

Miles Murray Sorrell FUEL
Miles Murray Sorrell FUEL has existed as a design group since 1991, when the principals were students at the Royal College of Art. Over the last ten years, they have forged regular relationships with clients, including Marc Jacobs, Levi's, and MTV. Two books about Miles Murray Sorrell FUEL are available: *Pure FUEL* (1996) by Booth-Clibborn Editions and *FUEL 3000* (2000) by Laurence King.

Miles Murray Sorrell FUEL
33 Fournier St.
Spitalfields
London E1 6QE UK
t. 020.7377.2697
f. 020.7247.4697
www.fuel-design.com

Hideki Nakajima, Nakajima Design
Hideki Nakajima was born in Saitama, Japan. Educated in Tokyo, he established Nakajima Design Inc., in 1995. He has won numerous Japanese and international awards for his work. He was involved with *Cut* magazine as a photographer and art director. His two books, *Revival* and *Nakajima Design 1995–2000*, are available through Rockin' On.

Hideki Nakajima
Nakajima Design Inc.
Kaiho Building 4F, 4-11
Uguisudani-cho
Shibuya-ku
Tokyo Japan 150-0032
t. 81.3.5489.1757
f. 81.3.5489.1758
nkjm-d2@kd5.se-net.ne.jp

Mark Randall, Worldstudio, Inc. and Worldstudio Foundation

Together with David Sterling, Mark Randall founded both Worldstudio, Inc., a design company, and Worldstudio Foundation, a nonprofit organization designed to connect designers with a variety of political causes. The latter publishes an annual magazine called *Sphere*, which showcases its projects with a wide range of work by international designers.

Mark Randall
Worldstudio, Inc.
225 Varick St., Floor 9
New York, NY 10014 USA
t. 212.366.1317 ext. 11
f. 212.807.0024
www.worldstudioinc.com
www.worldstudio.org

Stefan Sagmeister, Sagmeister Inc.

Stefan Sagmeister was born and trained in Austria. He worked for Leo Burnett in Hong Kong and now runs Sagmeister Inc., in New York City. His monograph, *Made You Look* (2000), is available from Booth-Clibborn Editions.

Sagmeister Inc.
222 W. 14 St., #15a
New York, NY 10011 USA
t. 212.647.1789
f. 212.647.1788
ssagmeiste@aol.com
www.sagmeister.com

Scott Santoro, Worksight Studio

Scott and his partner, Emily, have been working together as Worksight for over 12 years. They are both adjunct instructors at the Pratt Institute and have been active in the New York chapter of the American Institute of Graphic Artists. Scott's experience in corporate culture includes early employment at Landor Associates where he developed visual identities for national brands, and at Mobil Oil Corporation where he held the position of senior designer in charge of internal communications. In 1986, he returned to school to earn an M.F.A. in graphic design. Scott has also served for one year as treasurer ('98–'99), and two years ('99–'01) as vice president of the New York chapter of the AIGA. Emily holds a bachelor's degree in anthropology from Barnard College and applies this knowledge to the culture of graphic design. She is a visiting professor at Pratt Institute, teaching a visual communications course within the under-graduate graphic design B.F.A. program. Worksight designs are included in publications by *Etapes Graphiques* (France), *Graphics International* (England), *ID* magazine, *PBC International*, *Plus Eighty One* (Japan), *Art and Design* magazine (Beijing), and *Print* magazine. They have won awards from the AIGA, ACD, NY Bookbinders Guild, and *Print* magazine.

Worksight
46 Great Jones St.
New York, NY 10012 USA
t. 212.777.3558
f. 212.475.9098
www.worksight.com

Rudy VanderLans and Zuzana Licko, Emigre

Rudy VanderLans moved to California from the Netherlands in 1982 and studied photography at UC Berkeley, where he met the Czechoslovakian-born designer Zuzana Licko. They married in 1983. In 1984, they launched *Emigre* magazine. VanderLans and Licko were among the first designers to use the Macintosh computer as a tool. In addition to their quarterly magazine, Emigre creates and sells hundreds of digital typefaces. Nearly twenty years and sixty-four issues later, *Emigre* continues to fuel imaginations and inspire designers the world over.

Their company has been honored with numerous awards, including the 1994 Chrysler award for excellence in design and the 1998 Charles Nypels award for excellence in the field of typography. Emigre is also the recipient of the 1997 American Institute of Graphic Arts gold medal award and in 2000 they were nominated for the Cooper-Hewitt national design lifetime achievement award.

Emigre
4475 D St.
Sacramento, CA 95816 USA
t. 916.451.4344
f. 916.451.4351
www.emigre.com

Todd Waterbury, Wieden+Kennedy, New York

Todd joined Wieden+Kennedy in 1994 as an art director in the Portland, Oregon, office to help develop and launch the advertising, packaging, and promotion for Coca-Cola's "OK Soda." Promoted to creative director on Coca-Cola, his responsibilities included global campaigns for Diet Coke, Brand Coke Olympics, and Barq's. His role expanded to oversee the brand advertising for Microsoft. Since then, Todd has been instrumental in helping win the PowerAde business with the "Very Real Power" campaign. In 2001, Todd moved to lead the agency's New York office, partnering with co-creative director Ty Montague.

Prior to joining Wieden+Kennedy, Todd worked as an art director and designer at Fallon McElligott/Duffy Group in Minneapolis on assignments for Giorgio Armani, Porsche, and Jim Beam Brands, followed by two years at Bloomingdale's in New York as the executive art director responsible for storewide event advertising, package design, and brand identity.

In addition to best-of-category medals from D&AD, The Art Directors Club, and *ID*, Todd's work has appeared in the international publications of *Eye*, *Archive*, and *IDEA* as well as the *New York Times'* op ed column. His work is part of the permanent collections of the Victoria & Albert Museum in London, the San Francisco Museum of Modern Art, the Museum of Modern Art in New York, and his parents' family room in Macomb, Illinois.

Todd Waterbury
Wieden+Kennedy
150 Varick St., Floor 7
New York, NY 10019 USA
t. 917.661.5200
f. 917.661.5500
www.wk.com

About the author and designer

¶
About the author
Sarah Dougher
Sarah Dougher writes about graphic design when she is not teaching ancient civilization at colleges around the Pacific Northwest. In addition, she is the program manager at the Rock-n-Roll Camp for Girls in Portland and tours internationally with her rock bands. Her other published works include *XXX: The Power of Sex in Contemporary Graphic Design* and *Sent Out on the Tracks They Built: Sinophobia in Olympia, 1885*. She is also a recording artist for Mr. Lady records. She can be contacted at sarahdougher@hotmail.com.

¶
About the designer
Joshua Berger
Joshua Berger is a founding member and one of three principals of Plazm. He serves as managing partner and co-creative director for the firm. Berger has been recognized by numerous design publications and award shows, among them the Art Director's Club, the Graphis annual, and AIGA national show. He received the Gold Medal at the Leipzig Bookfair for his collaboration with John C Jay on the book *Soul of the Game*, published in 1998 by Melcher Media/Workman. His most recent projects include development of the Web site www.anti-war.us, dedicated to distribution of anti-war graphics, assignments for Jantzen, Nike, and branding for Pierce Brosnan. He designed and co-curated the book, *XXX: The Power of Sex in Contemporary Graphic Design*, published in 2003 by Rockport Publishers, and is at work on two new book projects. He can be reached at josh@plazm.com.

¶
Plazm
Founded in 1991 by artists as a creative resource, Plazm publishes an eclectic design and culture magazine with worldwide distribution and operates an innovative type foundry. Plazm is also a design firm that builds identities, advertising, interactive and retail experiences using custom typography. Plazm recently authored the book *XXX: The Power of Sex in Contemporary Design*, and is working on a new series of books about creative expression on the margins of culture. Current projects include a Plazm monograph, a twenty-plus variation customized global type identity for Nike, and a fourty-two color silkscreen print of The Last Supper and branding assignments for Pierce Brosnan.

In late 2002, Plazm launched the Web site www.anti-war.us to provide anti-war graphics free to activists globally.

Plazm was listed in 1997 in *ID* magazine as one of the world's 40 most influential design firms and has been featured in numerous publications and award shows including the 100 show, AIGA national show, the Art Director's Club, *Eye*, *Communication Arts*, *Graphis*, and *IDEA*. Plazm received the creative resistance award from *Adbusters* in 2001. Plazm partners regularly present work internationally, teach, create workshops and judge competitions. *Plazm* magazine has been published since 1991 and the complete catalog is included in the permanent collection of the San Francisco Museum of Modern Art.

Plazm partners are: Joshua Berger, Niko Courtelis, and Pete McCracken.

PLAZM
mail.   P. O. Box 2863
            Portland, OR 97208
            USA
ship.   1640 NW Johnson
            Portland, OR 97209
            USA
t.   503.528.8000
f.   503.528.8092
            design@plazm.com
            www.plazm.com

Acknowledgments
Thanks to the staff at Plazm: Jeremy Bittermann, Niko Courtelis, Pete McCracken, and Jon Raymond. Thanks to Tiffany Lee Brown for editing assistance.

Production Notes
This book and cover were printed in China by Midas Printing International Limited in process color with full aqueous coating on a Heidelburg sheet-fed press. Paper is 128GSM Japanese Matte Text.

Typography
Headlines and body text are set in Bitstream Futura.